> Joe Gossé, a native son of the Allentown diocese, was a committed Catholic in every way. He had a depth of spirit and a strong desire to always be the presence of Christ, especially with those on the margins of life.
> —**Most Reverend Alfred Schlert**
> Bishop of Allentown, PA, USA

> I first met Joseph Gossé in 1961 when he joined the Jesuits as a novice. I had just completed the two-year novitiate, but we got to know each other since we were both graduates of the Jesuit high school in Philadelphia. Later we lived and worked together, teaching at Gonzaga High School in Washington, D.C. Joe taught English and kept his quick wit lively for the rest of us young teachers. He was always smiling and it was a big loss when his sickness took him from the classroom. Eventually God led him to choose a vocation different from formal membership as a Jesuit, but he never forgot us and his Jesuit ideals. God blessed his dozen years as a Jesuit and that blessing never left him.
> —**Father George Burr, S.J.**
> Retired president of St. Joseph's Prep, Philadelphia, and former assistant to the president of St. Joseph's University, USA

A simple phrase by Joe once changed my life for the better and forever. There may very well be something in this book that will change yours. You in turn can be a new spark of life-giving wisdom for many others in your circle. My friendship with Joe was wrapped around knowing him almost 30 years. Yet it was one thing he said in conversation that most profoundly affected my life. My challenge is that you find at least that one pearl of great price between this front and back cover.
—**Rita Pursel**
Spiritual director, retired
St. Francis Friary, Easton, PA, USA

Joe Gossé and I became friends during the ten years before his death. He was immersed in such a wide variety of community and ecclesial endeavors. I was most struck by his understanding of suffering. Joe's Job-like reflections on human suffering during our many conversations were replete with inspiration for untold souls—locally, nationally, and internationally. His personal health and medical infirmities led him to project a unique and universal compassion and resource of hope amidst everyone's pain. He once confided at a lunch together, "I no longer see that success is the more worthy goal than failure. Rather, our utmost aim in life must be completing our journey in the midst of suffering."
—**Gerald Stover**
Lay ecumenist, Bethlehem, PA, USA

CONVERSATIONS WITH JOE

PRACTICAL WISDOM FOR EVERY DAY

Edited by Ron Shegda
Foreword by Archbishop Joseph E. Kurtz

Leonine Publishers
Phoenix, Arizona

Copyright © 2019 Ron Shegda

All rights reserved. No part of this book may be reproduced or transmitted in any form or by any means, electronic or mechanical, including photocopying, recording, or by any information storage or retrieval system now existing or to be invented, without written permission from the respective copyright holder(s), except for the inclusion of brief quotations in a review.

Published by
Leonine Publishers LLC
Phoenix, Arizona, USA

ISBN-13: 978-1-942190-48-6
Library of Congress Control Number: 2018967542
Printed in the United States of America
10 9 8 7 6 5 4 3 2 1

Visit us online at www.leoninepublishers.com
For more information: info@leoninepublishers.com

DEDICATION

Ad Maiorem Dei Gloriam
To the Greater Glory of God
—*Saint Ignatius of Loyola*

CONTENTS

Dedication..v

Foreword.. xi
by Archbishop Joseph E. Kurtz

Preface xiii
Ron Shegda

Acknowledgements............................... xix

Introduction: For Joe, With Love 1
Ron Shegda

Sunday
The Sabbath as Pause

Morning Worship...................................9
Monsignor Alfred R. Ott

Rediscovering the Family 19
Joe Gossé

Community & Scripture.......................... 24
Father Larry Hess

Monday
A New Workweek

The Spirituality of Work 35
Deacon Dr. William F. Urbine

Midday Rest 49
Joe Gossé

Evening Study: Becoming Conversant with the
Subject 55
Tom Gossé

Tuesday
Listening

Listening to Clients 61
Bishop Ronald W. Gainer

Afternoon Work Break: Breaking into Prison 66
Diane Varra, Msgr. Juan Grabish, Fr. Juanito Gibbons, Malena Cecelia Gallardo Díaz, Ron Shegda

Evening Work: Writing to Congress 71
Ed Delviscio

Wednesday
A Hard Man Is Good to Find

Driving the Congressman 77
Dr. Don Ritter

Quiet Tenacity 83
Rev. John Gibbons

Nighttime Entertainment: Walker, Texas Ranger ... 87
Joe Gossé

Thursday
Deepening the Spirituality of Work

The Work of Writing 95
Ron Shegda

Recreation as Re-creation 102
Rita Pursel

Contents

Driving My Son from Practice 107
Joe Gossé

Friday
Long Days, Hard Nights

Deeper Conversations: Universal Time 115
Tom Gossé

Fast Lunch.. 130
Rev. Thomas J. Orsulak

The Spirituality of Marriage...................... 131
Mary Clare Gossé
Todd and Karen Benckini

Saturday
Thank God It's Saturday

Go East, Young Man 155
Father Joe Lacey, S.J.

Inexhaustible Springs............................ 160
Joe Gossé

Friendship, Marriage, and a Community of Love .. 169
Robert A. Campanella

Epilogue 1 175
Tim Benckini, son of Joe Gossé
Roxine Susan Simms, daughter of Joe Gossé

Epilogue 2: Prayer to Saint Joseph................ 179

Notes.. 181

FOREWORD

— *by Archbishop Joseph E. Kurtz*

It has been years since I last saw Joe Gossé, Jr., and yet I pictured him when I recently read *Gaudete et Exultate*. This apostolic exhortation by Pope Francis, promulgated on the Feast of Saint Joseph, March 19, 2018, speaks of Joe's spirit. Near the end, Pope Francis writes, "Let us ask the Holy Spirit to pour out upon us a fervent longing to be saints for God's greater glory, and let us encourage one another in this effort" (n. 177). Anyone who ever met and became a friend of Joe Gossé would quickly say, "That captures Joe!"

In the summer of 1971 as newly ordained deacon, I started my assignment at St. Joseph parish in Limeport, Pennsylvania. Possibly the first parishioner I met was Joe Gossé, Sr. He was serving the parish as a catechist, and his warm, soft voice was just the welcome I needed to begin public ministry in the Church. Soon, I visited him and his dear and sweet wife Peg in their home in Coopersburg and met two of their sons, Joe and Tommy. For the next 30 years, my life and that of the Gossé family would be intertwined. After priestly ordination, I spent two summers in Limeport and deepened my friendship with and love of this fine family. Then in the early 1980s, I found myself engaged in ministries that would help me deepen even more my friendship with Joe, Jr.

As I served as director of the Diocesan Social Action Bureau, reaching out to those who were poor and vulnerable, Joe was there to help. We obtained grants to provide Catholic adults an understanding of the two pastoral letters from the U.S. bishops, on the challenge of peace and on the economy, and Joe was there. I recall traveling in crammed cars to teach the seminars. Joe was there and brought enthusiasm, a love of Jesus and His Church, a natural knack for supporting others, and—yes—wisdom.

The chapters of this book reveal a rich tapestry that tells a story. Again, Pope Francis captures the theme well: "The saints surprise us, they confound us, because by their lives they urge us to abandon a dull and dreary mediocrity" (n. 138). See if the chapters that follow don't surprise, confound, and lift you from mediocrity.

> **—Most Reverend Joseph E. Kurtz, D.D., Archbishop of Louisville**
> *24 June 2018, Solemnity of the Birth of Saint John the Baptist*

PREFACE

A dear friend of many, Joe Gossé passed away at 3:30 in the morning, September 26, 2000. "Well done! Good and faithful servant. Come, share your Master's joy" (Matthew 25:21).

Joe always liked the Parable of the Silver Pieces, the origin of this verse. As a financial advisor, he delighted in the practical ways of bringing the Gospel to ordinary life. And he loved ordinary life, the ordinary seasons of the Church.

Joe saw the ordinary wherever he was. He represented how our native genius shows us an extra experience of the ordinary. Thereby the ordinary becomes *extra*-ordinary. First he was alongside his beloved wife, Mary Clare, his "diva." He was a devoted father to Tim, Todd, and Roxine. To Joe it was ordinary to serve the hungry at ecumenical soup kitchens or share Sunday's Scripture readings with the incarcerated at Lehigh County Prison in Pennsylvania. Quite regularly, Joe and Mary opened their home to a Scripture sharing among friends. Joe lived the corporal and spiritual works of mercy. Stations in life did not influence Joe's sense of the ordinary. To him, serving on the staff of a United States congressman or consulting with a cardinal archbishop was no different than a Sunday afternoon chat with a friend. Joe knew how to enter into the mind and heart of another.

I often told Joe and Mary that Christ Jesus was very present in their lives. After all, they were Joseph and Mary, with Jesus between them.

This book, while a tribute to Joe, brings his practical wisdom before the everyday lives of a wide audience. In fact, that's how the chapters are organized: according to the days of the week. Joe possessed numerous Gospel-rich ways of living each part of the day. This book allows the reader to journey with Joe through moments of his "ordinary" days, giving us the opportunity for learning and emulation. It's actually written by all sorts of people who knew Joe.

American Founder Benjamin Franklin, who lived in Joe's and my native Philadelphia, wrote something pertinent in his *Autobiography*. The sage from the "City of Brotherly and Sisterly Love" said this: "If you want a book written about you, either do things worth writing about, or write things worth repeating." Joe scored a perfect tally on both standards.

Hopefully this writing inspires every reader that Servants of God cross our everyday lives all the time. Maybe that Servant of God is one day us. "Servant of God" is a designation by the Catholic Church for a departed soul who lived a holy life. It's a beginning step of a more formal heavenly journey through veneration, beatification, then canonization. The lay faithful should be cautioned that it is not our province to canonize anyone—only the Church may declare sainthood. Yet the Feast of All Saints' Day, every November 1 on the Roman Calendar, remains an invitation that each of us aspire to be saints. After all, saints are sinners who never gave up.

Similarly with the designation of Servant of God, only the Church may declare such a title. Did Joe Gossé live a life worthy of this memory? Every reader may gain a glimpse for him or herself.

Joe knew how to make a friend, be a friend, and lead that friend more intimately to Christ. I first met Joe in 1990. Our men's group at St. Ann parish in Emmaus, Pennsylvania, was conducting our annual Lenten series on spiritual topics. That year it was "The Shroud of Turin." My role—you guessed it—was communications leader. I began calling nearby parishes for placing bulletin announcements. The famed Shroud would be of interest for the faithful near and wide. When Father Harry Strassner from neighboring St. Paul parish in Allentown (whom I knew from Cursillo) answered the phone, he said: "Sure. Send it over." I concluded the conversation by asking, "Father, is there anyone at St. Paul's interested in 'social justice'?"—as I was active with our Diocesan Social and Economic Justice Speakers' Bureau.

Father Harry did not hesitate. He said, "We have Joe Gossé as a parishioner. I'm sure he's your man." Joe and I met within a short period of time and exchanged our current writing. Joe was an immensely better writer than me. From that first moment of warm smiles and handshakes at my home, Joe became a close friend until the day he passed away. I was so grateful to see him a few hours before he closed his eyes to this world—at 57 years young. Joe was the wisest and most educated person I ever knew as a close personal friend. His wisdom was outshone only by his unassuming humility.

The summer before Joe died, he began a dialogue with me about another book. He wanted us to write something together about our educational histories. In these present pages, Joe's idea follows its own course. This volume here draws the reader "to listen" in on a conversation with and about Joe's life, for meaningful self-insight. As I worked with family and friends of Joe, recreating these "conversations" through vignettes and notes, everyone could all hear Joe say, "We should make haste slowly." But he would say it in Latin!

I will provide an introduction for each section of this book. Therein, I will introduce both the topic and writer. In some sections we read Joe's own words—from his pure heart and brilliant mind. All other contributors are either members of Joe's family, intimate friends, or former colleagues.

When Joe lay in his casket, a lifeless hand clutched a still life-giving Rosary. Joe well understood in this valley of tears that when we seek the presence of Jesus, a way of certainty is going first to Mary, His mother. God sent Jesus to this world through Mary at

Preface

the Annunciation. Jesus entrusted Mary to Saint John and to us at the cross. Joe knew that when we need Jesus—which is always—at any moment of life or upon grave difficulty, we can find Him through Mary. *Ad Jesum per Mariam*—To Jesus through Mary. Or as Archbishop Fulton J. Sheen observed, when we meet Jesus and seek entry into Heaven, He will say: "Come. Enter. My Mother has spoken well of you."

— *Ron Shegda*

ACKNOWLEDGEMENTS

Tim Benckini is the oldest son of Joe and Mary Clare. He and his wife Leona live in Pennsylvania's Lehigh Valley with their two teen sons. Tim graduated with a BS in Business and Political Science from St. Francis DeSales University.

Todd and Karen Benckini live in Maryland with their teenage twins, Joe and Georgiana. Todd earned an MBA at DeSales University. Karen holds a degree from Loyola University—a Jesuit school.

Bob Campanella lives with his wife Linda and their two children in Laurys Station, PA. He's an engineer with a large corporation.

Ed Delviscio is a school guidance counselor. He and his wife Diane reside in Bethlehem with their children nearby.

The Most Reverend Ronald W. Gainer is Catholic bishop of Harrisburg, PA.

Rev. John Gibbons serves as a priest of Pennsylvania's Allentown diocese. He is pastor of Sacred Heart parish, Allentown, PA.

Mary Clare Gossé holds a Doctorate in Education from Temple University. Dr. Gossé resides in Pennsylvania's Lehigh Valley.

Tom Gossé and his wife Jean live in The Woodlands, TX. They have three adult children. Tom Gossé retired early from a career in computer software. Their two sons are Thomas and Charles. Their eldest daughter Tara lives in Pennsylvania. Joe was older brother to Tom.

Rev. Larry Hess worked as a priest in the Allentown diocese. He was pastor of two parishes, entering eternity February 21, 2014.

The Most Reverend Joseph E. Kurtz was ordained a priest in the Allentown diocese in 1972. He previously met the Gossé family when assigned as deacon to the parish of St. Joseph in Limeport, PA, in 1971. Archbishop Kurtz has served as the fourth archbishop of Louisville, KY, since 2007.

Rev. Joe Lacey, S.J., served as pastor of a parish in Woodstock, MD. He and Joe attended St. Joseph's Preparatory School together in Philadelphia in the 1960s.

Monsignor Thomas J. Orsulak has served several parishes and educational ministries in the Allentown diocese.

Monsignor Alfred R. Ott was rector of Joe's parish, the Cathedral Church of St. Catharine of Siena, until retirement in 2003. He passed into eternity October 31, 2014, the eve of All Saints' Day.

Rita Pursel and her husband Joseph live in Hellertown, PA. She worked as a spiritual director and retired from the staff of the St. Francis Retreat House in Easton, PA.

ACKNOWLEDGEMENTS

Dr. Don Ritter consults on international and environmental issues in Washington, D.C. He was Pennsylvania's 15th Congressional District representative from 1979 to 1993. Joe initially served as special assistant then as a legislative aide to Don.

Roxine Susan Simms is the daughter of Joe and Mary Clare Gossé and is married to Jimmy Simms. She earned her Masters in Rehabilitation Counseling at Texas Tech University. They live in Texas.

Deacon Dr. William F. Urbine and his wife Christine are members of St. Paul's parish, Allentown, PA, surrounded by their children and grandchildren. He is director of Family Life Ministries for the Allentown diocese.

Diane Varra is a member of St. Paul's Catholic parish in Allentown, PA, and coordinates the Lehigh County Prison Ministry.

INTRODUCTION: FOR JOE, WITH LOVE

Joe rarely spoke of his multiple, grave medical complications, present for decades. Many of his friends never even knew he had lived for a year at home without ingesting a morsel of food or letting any liquid pass his lips. He survived that year in 1997 on home intravenous feeding. You would never know it. He ran a full complement of regular appointments. Talk about Jesus hanging on the cross and saying, "I thirst." Joe certainly knew Jesus on the cross.

Joe loved the Carmelite order and frequently wrote for two Carmelite publications. The Carmelites are one of the more austere, cloistered religious congregations in the Catholic fold. Saint Teresa of Avila, a 16th century Spanish reformer of this order of priests and nuns—along with her confessor and Joe's favorite Carmelite, Saint John of the Cross—wrote about souls like Joe: "We always find that those who walk closest with Christ suffer the greatest trials."

Just as many of us, Joe quivered several "go to" saints in his repertoire. We see here one of them was Saint John of the Cross, 16th century Spanish Carmelite priest, confessor, spiritual director, and reformer of his religious order with his friend, Saint Teresa of Avila. (Few know that Saint John of the Cross is regarded as a poet laureate by the nation of Spain.) Joe often wrote articles for Carmelite periodicals, including *Spiritual Life* and *Living Prayer.*

Joe supplemented easily obtainable pearls by this nationally recognized literary great of Spanish culture. For instance, Saint John's feast day—December 14—as quoted in *The Liturgy of the Hours*, says to the effect that "we can only achieve holiness by entering into the thicket of suffering."[1] Joe went on to tell various vignettes from the life of Saint John. On one occasion, this saint confiscated the rosary of one his penitents. He firmly concluded that she was worshiping her rosary beads as if they had some magical power—instead of being a direct conduit of Scriptural prayer and reflection upon the mysteries of Jesus' life as witnessed by the Mother of God, the Blessed Virgin Mary. After all, there has *never* been anything in Mary's life that was not completely of God.

Joe also liked to reiterate Saint John of the Cross' Gospel admonition of wariness about anyone who suddenly appears in the Name of Jesus. (See Matthew 7:15–20, along with other passages.) Saint John was clear, as Joe liked to relay. If a charlatan traipses into town claiming to speak for Jesus, our saint would slip out of Dodge, headed the other way.

During that year of imposed fasting travail, Joe would come to our regular lunch get-togethers and

Introduction: For Joe, with Love

simply feast on the conversation. When Sunday later came, he would enjoy afternoon talks with his family members or with friends on the telephone. Of course he was faithful to Sunday morning Mass. When I once asked why he did not attend weekday liturgies, he said, "A little salt goes a long way." It is not quite true that he did not take part in weekday liturgy. Joe was faithful to praying the Liturgy of the Hours. Sometimes while driving, he would have his breviary popped open on the passenger seat. Nuggets of Scripture awaited him at red lights.

Joe liked telling the story, from years ago, when a woman spotted him carrying his Bible in an elevator. She said, "I see you carry your sword with you." Joe had a deep reverence for the Scriptures. He was once interviewed on a local radio station. I could not pass up the opportunity during the call-in portion. After introducing myself, I asked Joe what priority he would commend that young people follow for growth: *A spiritual director? Courses in theology? Or study of the Scriptures?* In his wry way, he quipped, "What is this, a quiz?" Then he answered, "If I had to choose one, it would be knowing the Scriptures. Yet they are all important."

Joe employed a coterie of probing questions once he gained the trust of someone new, especially a younger adult embarking on life's journey: *What is your philosophy? What is your religion?* For his own religious faith, Joe nurtured a deep devotion to the Sacred Heart of Jesus.

When I would take him to dialysis or visit him during his numerous times in the hospital, he filled my mind and heart with the most wonderful thoughts. Like Mary, the Mother of God, he pondered so many mysteries of Christ and humanity in his brilliant soul. Even in passing, Joe remains a light to many.

If you ever asked Joe the topic of his many published articles, he would say "family and Scripture." Following is an excerpt from his article, "Contemplative Chore," published in *Living Prayer* magazine. It was about his son Todd. He published articles about all of his children. He loved to speak about the turning point in the relationship with his younger son referenced in this article. It was when Todd first asked Joe how his day had gone.

> I used to kindle interest with Todd through the choice of certain anecdotes from my own day. When we first started our conversations, my interjections had to be very brief. Todd was interested in sports or an event at school and wanted to get back to that as quickly as possible . . . Todd might ask a question or make a comment about my experience. One day he got into the car and asked me about my day. I knew we were turning a corner . . . My interest in Todd and his activities developed in him a capacity for interest in some of my work and

concerns. Two-way conversation was now a reality.

Yahweh lures us and leads us out into the wilderness in order to talk with us. He begins by speaking to our concerns, but gradually He leads us out to concerns and areas that are strange and different. What often begins as more of a chore turns little by little into the mutual interest of friends who really care for one another and for the concerns they are willing to share. A river is running through the desert.

He always had a good book in hand. He read widely and he read the best literature. Ever since we first met in 1990, no one person has more profoundly influenced my pattern of thought or base of knowledge. As part of a "group reunion" within the confines of the Cursillo Movement for several years, Joe took special interest in the dilemmas of those of us who gathered for lunch. He was exceptional at asking penetrating questions that would loosen self-insights. His published booklet, *Unemployed Workers*,[2] took shape at these luncheons. He delighted in reporting the work's progress solely as a way of helping anyone we knew who was unemployed. He understood that the other four at our table each passed through that gate at one point or another.

Joe reveled in the significance of personal influence. He treasured sharing the impact Jesuit Father William Lynch had on his intellectual and spiritual development. As a layperson, Joe held a deep affection of support for men serving as Catholic priests.

He likewise knew he possessed a power in fostering growth for others with one-on-one relationships. In the spring of 1999, he proposed a book called *Conversations* that the two of us would write. Kind of a *Tuesdays with Morrie*, the idea was to tape record and transcribe our questions, answers, and comments to each other regarding our educational histories. The audience would be younger people in encouragement of better lighting their own educational paths. I recorded a few of Joe's thrilling voice mails as a preface for the project now bequeathed to me.

Joe and I loved our voice mail repartee. For years we carried on conversations back and forth totally on voice mail. Joe listened to everything. He made people realize that we should measure our words. He would examine and respond to everything that was said. One of the greatest lessons Joe taught me was that "listening" is the highest expression of love.

I knew Joe's father, Joe Sr., before I knew Joe. Joe the elder was a saint, a kind and humble man, so easy with conversation. I was glad to have seen Joe the elder just before he passed away. Lying in his hospital bed, he spoke about the specialness of women. "Ronnie," he said, "women should never be like men." Later on, Joe the younger's brother, Tom, said their father was always consistent. His last comment to me just before he died, Tom confirmed, came from the loving regard

Introduction: For Joe, with Love

Joe the elder had for their mother, Margaret, whom I never met.

Apples usually fall close to the tree. Joe the younger is also a saint. He taught me a rejoinder to his father's parting outlook: "The two most important words between a man and woman are not 'Yes, Dear.'" "No," Joe said wisely, "the two most important words are 'Yes' and 'No.'" After all, Jesus, Saint Paul, and Saint James each say something to this effect. (See Matt. 5:37, James 5:12, and 2 Cor. 1:18–19.) We do not want peace at any price. We want husbands and wives who know and love *themselves* and *then* each other.

I was glad to have seen Joe a week before he died. Through Cursillo I knew how to give an *abrazzo*, a holy hug. I did so to Joe. I was running late with errands that Saturday and Joe let me know it. I thanked him so much for teaching me that "a hard man is good to find." Joe was hard in that he would not tolerate incongruence—saying two different things or not having your actions match your words. Joe stood for integrity, for doing what you say, practicing what you preach. If not, don't say anything. This quote about a "hard man" packs a wallop for manhood today. It also speaks volumes for any relationship to a man.

Let me supplement Joe's insights about "integrity" with a comparison to "honesty." They are opposite sides of the same coin. Integrity is doing what you say; honesty is saying what you do.

The summer before Joe died, he called to say his beloved Jesuit friend, Father Bill Dych, S.J., had just passed away. He told me we had good advocates at the Throne: Bill Dych and William Lynch. When my mentor Bob Rodale was tragically killed in 1990, it was Joe who called and listened for at least half an hour about Bob's influence on me and upon our world today. Joe said that "regeneration" had a new advocate at the Throne.

From the pages that follow, despite the loss of such an exceptional conversationalist, let us find joy in believing that Heaven has gained a saint. He is someone who leaves behind a bright legacy: practical wisdom for every day.

Well done, good and faithful servant. Share your Master's joy. Please pray for us, Joe, as we try to follow the Christ whom you revealed for our journey home. To the Greater Glory of God—*Ad Maiorem Dei Gloriam*.

— *Ron Shegda*

CHAPTER 1
SUNDAY
THE SABBATH AS PAUSE

Morning Worship

Joe was a deeply spiritual man. Describing him as "religious" would not accurately capture his humble simplicity or deep complexity. Joe did not preach in the televangelist sense. You might engage in a dozen conversations with him over several months and never hear the names God, Jesus, or Holy Spirit. Yet you knew he possessed a deep and living faith. A persistent preference for identifying his religion was passing you an article he wrote for Spiritual Life Magazine *or* Living Prayer. *Or he might hand you a book, or a copy of* Family Magazine *that said something about your interests.*

There was one stretch of time when I was wondering if Joe would ever say something explicitly about the Christian faith. Then in the course of a conversation, when he was speaking about mentoring someone, he said: "Ron, there comes a moment when you have to ask: 'What's your philosophy? What's your religion?'" It made me realize Joe cared profoundly about religious faith.

After a number of years, I wondered why Joe never saw the need to attend daily Mass. Again he answered pointedly: "Ron, a little salt goes a long way." That was it. He simply meant that—for him—Sunday worship provides enough spiritual energy for the entire week. "Conversing" with Joe through this book, discovering how he represented and modeled each day of the week, and different parts of each day, all have their beginning point in Sunday morning—the first day of the week.

In total this book is a week with Joe. It represents how he lived that eternal rhythm of God's seven days of creation and redemption.

— Ron Shegda

Joe and Mary Clare were members of the Cathedral Church of St. Catharine of Siena, Allentown, when I was pastor. Joe was a lector. He was also very active with the Allentown Serra Club, in support of priestly vocations. I was chaplain at the time. So I got to know Joe through my pastoral duties.

Two things stand out most about Joe. First, I think of him in relationship with the desert. The other point about Joe concerns his proclaiming the Word at Sunday morning worship.

Concerning this first dimension, deserts are dry, without life. For sustaining life, you need water. Life in the desert means finding water. Joe had a characteristic similar to the ancient Israelites after the Exodus. They dug wells deep into the earth for sustaining themselves and their flocks. Many people, however, live lives on a dry, sandy surface. They neglect searching for the deep wells of life in their minds, hearts, and souls. Joe knew how to mine the depth of his own person. He lived to mine meaning in the world where we all live. Once he found the source of water, it bubbled up and renewed himself and anyone with whom he entered into a dialogue. Joe searched for and found life-giving waters.

That's the way Joe approached the Scriptures. Anyone listening when he lectured at Sunday Mass could tell how he was completely immersed in what he read. A certain experience from my ministry at St. Anne in Bethlehem alerted me to the way someone like Joe could find depth in the Scriptures. At that time there was a lot of ecumenical and interfaith activity. We were getting together with Protestant churches and synagogues. When the youth group at St. Anne met with a Jewish congregation, the young Jewish people showed us how they conduct a worship service and read the Scriptures. Of course, they read from the Torah in ancient Hebrew.

I asked the Jewish youngsters if they understood what they were reading. They reminded me of our own Catholic tradition when kids would memorize the Latin responses for Mass, but not really know what the words meant. They responded from memorization. It was the same with these young souls that day at the synagogue. Almost everyone confirmed they didn't know what they were saying, but one Jewish boy spoke up: "I might not understand what I am saying, but in speaking these words, I am speaking the very words that God spoke. And the Scriptures tell me that is sweeter to the mouth than honey." He later told me that he always considered it a great honor and blessing to be able to use the very words by which God spoke to His people. [For instance, see Psalm 19:10–11: "The ordinances of the Lord are true, all of them just . . . Sweeter also . . . than syrup or honey from the comb."]

Whenever Joe and I had a conversation, he was very humorous. That was part of his holiness and his sanctity. These virtues intertwined with his gift of simplicity, which God gave him. So many misunderstand the virtue of simplicity. Simplicity is beautiful. Yet we're such a complex society. Nothing is simple anymore. For instance, families don't have TVs anymore; they have entertainment centers. And there's not one button to push, but dozens on four remotes. Or consider driving a car. Putting the key in the ignition [and now it's carrying a transponder!] is so simple; but figuring out what's under the hood can make your head spin. Simplicity means not having a whole lot of parts where you have to be concerned. The idea of simplicity is dealing with a *whole*—while perhaps appreciating all its many parts, but not being an "expert" on every detail.

When Joe spoke, he did so with a real simplicity. His words came from deep within himself, from his heart. His conversations were like that deep well bubbling up from the desert. He had things to say that resulted from his intimate union with God, with Christ. And when you think about it, water is very simple. It's H2O. Water is a simple chemical compound. Yet we can't live without water. Water reminds us that we can't live without simplicity.

At the same time, water has a certain diversity and complexity to it. Water freezes and becomes ice. It heats up and becomes vapor. We see water in rain and dew. There's fresh water and salt water, supporting all sorts of different life. There's a water cycle. This "complexity" of water originates in its great *diversity*. But fundamentally water remains simple. This better depicts Joe. He was so diverse from his many interests and talents. However, at heart he showed that life can be as simple as telephoning a friend on a Sunday afternoon. Whether the day was sun-drenched or rain-soaked, Joe loved giving someone a call or writing them a letter.

The "complex" dimension of Joe's intellect sprang from his Jesuit education. The Jesuits like the idea of "casuistry"—seeing all the different angles of some problem or situation. That's what makes something complex: the various angles. Reason enlightened by faith helps us distinguish the greater and the lesser, the cause and the effect, the whole and the parts. That sums up Joe's depth as a person. He was a very simple person. At the same time, due to the many diverse dimensions of his personhood, you might mistake him for being complex.

In this way Joe was very close to God. God Himself is both simple and complex. He came to earth as the baby Jesus. What is more simple than a baby? Yet try understanding the Trinity, as Saint Augustine with his story of the little boy using a bucket for transferring the ocean into a hole on the beach: it's impossible to comprehend with our finite minds.

I knew Joe as his pastor. I'd speak with him before Mass if he was lectoring, or at a Serra Club dinner or meeting. Even though we didn't get together one-on-one or for lunch, it was easy to grasp Joe's magnanimity. For instance, Joe lectored—meaning he proclaimed either the First or Second Reading at Mass—because Vatican Council II encouraged that lay people become more active in liturgy. After all, "liturgy" means "work of the people." I noticed that some lectors were very well prepared. Others did not show much responsibility for their ministry. One key was how pastors trained the laity for proclaiming the Word, especially those who had no previous experience in public speaking. Yet the majority of parishes, from my view, never did that. They would just let someone get up there and read from the Lectionary. They never had them walk

Sunday: The Sabbath as Pause

around the church, listen to each other, or offer helpful guidance on doing better.

When I became pastor of the Cathedral parish in 1989, Joe was already a lector. Anyone listening realized Joe read with great understanding. He was skilled in delivering a complex series of words. For instance, if you read the Letters of Saint Paul, some of his sentences go on for miles. But Joe was able to read these passages so they made sense. It was very clear that Joe made significant preparations for the Readings at Sunday morning worship.

Going back to that Jewish boy at the synagogue, it was evident that Joe was not just "reading something." Many people adopt the approach: "I have to get up there and do a Reading." Or maybe one Sunday morning someone gets a shoulder tap: "The lector didn't show up. Would you like to read?" And the response comes, "Oh, sure. I'll go up and read." But the problem is someone at the lectern looking at the Reading for the first time. It was obvious that Joe prepared a week ahead. Just imagine if an ordinary parishioner was suddenly tapped on the shoulder to do a Sunday Mass Reading—and had actually prepared on his or her own during the week! While this is not usual, it should be the norm! We should all be prepared for Sunday worship.

Joe loved our Catholic priests. After all, he had himself aspired to the priesthood as a younger man. He always treated me with great reverence. As I reflected earlier, Joe brought humor to the Church. He saw the humorous side of our priests, of people. There was a certain sharpness to his humor. When a zinger was coming, he'd give you a hint by smiling. That smile let you prepare that something was coming. Then your memory of his smile would take the edge off something he told you that was very penetrating. Afterward, he'd give you a little "a-hem"—a feign of clearing his throat as if his humorous dart scored a bull's-eye.

For instance, a certain priest-friend was given a change of assignments and felt dejected. Joe assessed the situation. A gleam came to his eye. He smiled and said, "Just remember. Paul of Tarsus 'fired' John Mark from his missionary job and hired Silas instead. And John Mark went on to write the earliest Gospel. A-hem!" [Joe referred to Acts 15:36–41.]

At our Serra Club meetings, Joe loved working the crowd. He'd enjoy speaking with everyone. He loved listening to people, and he always had something meaningful to say. Joe was gregarious. If he never met you before, he'd figure out a way to strike up a conversation and put you at ease. Joe loved our priests because he loved our High Priest, Jesus Christ. He knew that without Christ, there would be no Church, no Gospel, no Eucharist, no Sunday worship. He supported the formation of priestly vocations and he supported priests through friendship during the week. He clearly connected Sunday with Monday by helping many priests, deacons, and religious with

Sunday: The Sabbath as Pause

their financial planning and retirement needs. After all, he worked as a licensed financial planner the last ten years of his life.

We all live in a weekly framework. God set up a pattern of six days for working and one day for rest. Christ then renewed that universal and eternal rhythm by His Resurrection. The Jewish Sabbath and day of rest—Saturday—was transformed on the first Easter morning. Sunday, the first day of the week, became the Christian Sabbath—properly the Lord's Day—through the mystery of God's Incarnation, Emmanuel, God Among Us. Joe understood this and lived this. Sunday liturgy was the beginning and propeller of his new week.

On occasion I would see Joe at daily Mass. He and Mary Clare were foremost fixtures at the Cathedral on Sunday morning. Of course, their children were all adults by the time I was their pastor. Moreover, Joe was a rare bird in understanding the relationship and continuum of the Liturgy at Mass and the Liturgy of the Hours. Joe loved his Breviary—the ancient collection of Scripture Readings and prayers throughout the day and night. He realized that Mass and the Liturgy of the Hours were part of one whole: they reflect heavenly worship of God the Father, God the Son, and God the Holy Ghost.

If you asked Joe when he had time to pray the Divine Office (or Liturgy of the Hours) amidst his hectic family and business schedule, he might share a personal secret. "Well, I keep my Breviary propped open to the appropriate hour on the passenger seat while driving. Then at stop lights, I'll pray a few verses of a Psalm." He especially loved Psalm 119 from the Midday or Midafternoon prayers—a Psalm extolling the love of the Law, the love of God's Word. Wow. Talk about living a life of prayer!

Joe simply and profoundly connected weekly Sunday worship and the Liturgy of the Hours with the entire liturgical year. He accurately knew that Sunday relates to the week as Easter relates to the year. Every Sunday is a "little Easter." We celebrate our Lord's redemption of sin and death for all of us. Holy Week was a most significant time for Joe. And he was always available as a lector during the Sacred Triduum—those holiest of Christian days encompassing Holy Thursday, Good Friday, Holy Saturday, and the Easter Vigil. Joe realized that each of these liturgies, which are actually all parts of a whole celebration, have their own special message and flavor.

In our time, Christmas is the big Feast, since that's when everyone seems to go to church. Easter has been relegated to "second best." Easter doesn't have the emotional appeal of a baby being born. Joe, as any good Christian, was counter-cultural. He saw Easter as the primary expression of Sabbath worship. He was very much like the boy in *The Little Prince*. He saw things clearly with his heart.[1]

— *Monsignor Alfred R. Ott*

SUNDAY: THE SABBATH AS PAUSE

Rediscovering the Family

No thinking person appreciates labels, especially for her- or himself. Labels box in free ideas. They box out creativity—keep you from thinking outside the box. Joe was a subscriber. He didn't like being characterized as a "religious writer." That title suggests a certain confinement that might narrow the audience. However, if you pressed Joe on the topics of his writing, he'd come out and say: Scripture and family.

That's why Joe was so tuned into the Sabbath. What sums up Sundays better than God's love letter to His people—the Bible—and reading and living those words of love with your family? Immersion in Scripture and family life on Sunday is precisely what led Joe to see "the Sabbath as pause." Whenever we take a 2, 5, or 15-minute break during the workweek for reflecting on a Bible verse or on the impulse of family love, we bring Sunday's peace into the accomplishment, pressure, or mayhem of work.

After all, isn't peace the mother of love? Thereby we allow Sunday—celebration of the Resurrection—to enter into whatever happens Monday through Saturday. Did we enjoy a great success on the job? Pausing in light of Sunday turns our gratitude toward God. Did someone hang up the phone on us? We identify with Jesus' passion. Or even during our "work" as parents or children, brothers or sisters, grandparents, or cousins: when we traipse in an hour late for dinner, the love shared from Sunday overcomes our disappointments.

While the other sections of this chapter give example for the importance of Scripture, especially on Sunday, Joe's writing below about family reveals his other great love. Now Joe was multi-dimensional and also loved his books and his friends. He almost equally treasured phoning a friend on a Sunday afternoon or re-reading one of his favorite authors. I remember visiting him one Sunday with my mother and sister at the Hospital of the University of Pennsylvania after an unsuccessful operation on his abdominal fistula. He was propped up on his bed, with a book in hand, and had a pile of seven or so books on the cart where his lunch should have been. Since he was being fed intravenously, Joe was free to feast on his books.

Tom Gossé identifies a number of Joe's favorite authors in Chapter 2. It's impossible to identify Joe as only a lover of the classics, or as an Anglophile, Francophile, or Italophile. French Catholic philosopher Gabriel Marcel, especially popular in the 1940s and '50s, was certainly in Joe's top five. So was England's G. K. Chesterton. Joe persistently referenced two of Professor Marcel's famous essays. They were both published in his 1951 English edition of Homo Viator *("The Traveling Man" or "Pilgrim Person"—which was a regular theme of Saint John Paul II the Great).*

One essay was titled "The Mystery of the Family." Marcel's other essay gets more evocative: "The Creative Vow as Essence of Fatherhood." Here we have Joe in his own words celebrating family life. Joe wrote this essay

Sunday: The Sabbath as Pause

for a 1992 edition of my publishing company's newsletter, New Generation News.

— *Ron Shegda*

Gilbert Keith Chesterton, a Catholic writer and thinker, once commented: "All truth comes through myth and fairy tale." With this arresting and paradoxical insight in mind, I wish to recall the ancient story of the sun and the wind.

It seems that one day the wind was boasting that he was more powerful than the sun. The sun politely declined any retort, so the wind set up a contest to prove his greater power. "Do you see that man traveling along the road with his cloak hung loosely about his shoulder?" the wind challenged the sun. "I'll bet I can get that cloak off his shoulders with my powerful breath." The sun smiled and the wind began to blow.

The gust of wind almost blew the man's cloak from his grasp. But when he felt the strong pull and the air becoming colder, he folded the cloak closer to himself and did not let go. The wind blew furiously but could not remove the man's cloak. Finally, the wind gave up.

The sun continued smiling. Her warmth and radiance gradually wrapped themselves around the traveler. The man loosened his grip and finally removed his cloak entirely, carrying it by his side.

This simple tale explains and illumines the truth about family in a way that would cheer Gilbert Chesterton. Encouragement, the warm radiance of relationship, is the fine context in which growth, change, and freely given response have their best opportunity to shine. The root meaning of *encourage* is "to give from one's heart"— an act which can draw out the best in people. The forceful focus on rules of conduct, the laws of living well, may certainly be correct and right. But, as with the power and challenge of the gusty wind, they may fail in their purpose.

Gabriel Marcel, a French Catholic philosopher, developed a philosophy of participation that forms a solid framework for encouragement within a family. In his reflections, he made a significant distinction between a *problem* and a *mystery*. A problem is external to ourselves; we treat it as something to be worked on, solved, and walked away from. We do not remain involved with the problem in a lasting way. Once we fix the car or repair the washing machine (and it really does not matter who works on it, just so it gets fixed), we can put our problem out of mind.

Marcel points out that a mystery, in the sense he uses the word, *involves us* as a person. We do not walk away from this mystery but rather participate and share in its reality *before* and *after* there is some kind of problem. Marcel reflects on the family as a mystery we experience instead of as a problem to be solved.

Marcel's vision of family is foundational for the lived experience of *our* family. He points us away from a running record of lawbreakers who require the exercise of power and retributive justice to behave.

Sunday: The Sabbath as Pause

Gabriel Marcel reflects on a living communion shared with one another. In this context, we work through the appreciation and gradual deepening of growth in the Law of Christ.

For example, we could find fault with a son or daughter, especially in their early years, at practically every turn in their road of growth. There is always a problem to correct or a law we can show they broke. Like the wind, we might feel our exercise of power should prevail for their change in attitude or behavior. Yet we experience a path of failure. We only see our children as problems.

This same daughter or son is the person we drive home from a practice or a game, or with whom we spend time watching television or just going for a Coke. These shared moments are opportunities. Since they are or can be repeated, they almost surely occur before and after "problems" arise. The conversations we can enjoy on these occasions are breeding grounds for encouragement, building blocks of trust. They nurture the creativity of relationship.

Commenting about a game or television program or a school activity, or simply listening without criticism or ridicule, slowly but surely, with time and repetition as resources, will acknowledge and celebrate the mystery of a family. Only within this context of such a living, breathing communion of persons will our expected problems really be solved, our family life find recovery, and our hope become refreshed.

— Joe Gossé

Community & Scripture

Joe and Mary loved gathering people in their home for studying the Scriptures. Joe loved the Bible. "Study" is not the best word for these evening get-togethers. They were more like a dreamy, timeless experience of complete enjoyment. Joe would lead everyone in "breaking open the Word." He'd help us find some meaningful phrase or verse, encourage us to make an insight, then ask that we share our understanding with everyone present. We were all free to mix and match our own self-discovery upon listening to God's voice.

Typically we would read Sunday's Gospel. While Sunday evening was the usual time for these occasional gatherings, Joe and Mary Clare were by no means doctrinaire with their invitations. Scripture sharing sometimes found a date on Friday or Saturday evening. Love is the greatest binding force of every family and any community. Joe taught that "the Scriptures are the greatest love letter ever written."

In Joe's glory years, after publishing his booklet on unemployed workers [2] and while having his simple paintings exhibited at Muhlenberg College in Allentown, he was the in-studio guest at a local radio talk show. Remember the caller from the Introduction who asked,

Sunday: The Sabbath as Pause

"What is your best advice for a young person—or anyone—looking for spiritual growth? Do you recommend studying theology? Finding a spiritual director? Or staying close to the Scriptures?" Very much in Joe Gossé fashion, he wryly answered, "Is this a quiz?" He then said, "All of these are good and worthwhile. Yet if I had to choose one, it would be the Scriptures."

Joe's facility with Scripture left a legacy for anyone gathered around him on making keen insights. For instance, in his compact volume on the unemployed, Joe saw that John Mark—writer of the Gospel of Mark—was "fired" by the Apostle Paul during their first missionary journey across the Mediterranean. A controversy arose where Mark, the young assistant to Paul and Barnabas, suddenly left and returned to Jerusalem. Later on, Paul insisted on keeping separate from Mark because "they should not take with them someone who had deserted them at Pamphylia and who had not continued with them in their work" (Acts 15:17–40). Perhaps in current sports lingo, John Mark had "taken a knee" to accent his position, which Paul did not accept!

In a certain way, Paul "hired a new executive secretary, Silas." This was how Joe reflected with others on ways the Scriptures are based on the lives of real people. They were also set to writing by real people. Joe encouraged that our imaginations in reading the Scriptures can give us a sense of context as to what was meaningful and practical within a certain Bible narrative.

It's also worth noting how Joe conveyed practical wisdom for any writing project. He used to advise, "Sometimes if you think you have a worthy manuscript for publication, put it on the shelf for ten years. Then get back to it for deciding what to do." That is exactly what happened with the publication of the first Gospel—written by Mark. It did not appear in written form until 30 years after the Resurrection of Jesus. Until then, all four Gospels only existed through oral tradition. John's Gospel itself, the fourth one transcribed, took another 30 years after Mark's.

In the "modern" world of internet blogs, posts, and texts that are typed in moments, such advice seems an anomaly. This present volume began by writing a eulogy upon Joe's passing in the year 2000. It then took the following 18 years until the completed work would find its way to a printing press.

— *Ron Shegda*

Joe and I were members of a "covenant community." That meant each and every member consciously recognized that our friendships were defined and bound by our Catholic Christian faith. We formed at the Allentown College of St. Francis de Sales (now DeSales University) in the 1970s. Named the "Children of Joy," our community sprang up from several "charismatic" retreats held for college students. Although I was a student, our growing community attracted a number of non-students, including Joe. Since the Oblate priests celebrated Mass every day at Wills Hall, people from surrounding towns joined college-connected people for worship. That's how I met Joe.

Joe was a lay theologian. He had been studying with the Jesuits at Fordham University and Georgetown University and wanted to be a Jesuit. Joe loved the Jesuits until his dying breath. Health reasons prompted his separation from Jesuit formation. As God would will, he was meant for Mary Clare, whom he got to know with the Children of Joy. They eventually married.

In the early 1970s Joe and I would hit The Brass Rail occasionally, a popular Allentown restaurant known for its cheese steaks. We'd talk theology. Theology, queen of all the sciences, is simply our faith in search of understanding. Theology is human reflection on the data of faith. And our faith is in God. Joe was great at theology. He had the gift—and he worked on developing that gift—of personalizing his theological insights for the friend (or stranger) with whom he was conversing. That's one of the ways he made friends and built community. He would take some profound truth, rooted in Scripture or Church teaching, and tell it to you in language you'd understand. He would also gently lead you, in the course of conversation, toward having you apply that truth to your own life.

After knowing Joe for a few years, I became a priest. So in my case, Joe would help me, often times at The Brass Rail, think through the Sunday Readings.

Our conversations would always benefit preparation for delivering my Sunday homily. Joe practiced reinforcing the spoken word with the written word. He would follow-up our conversations with carefully etched notes about the Bible Readings for Mass. His brief yet significant notes always ended with something like "Go Eagles" or "Go Phillies." (Joe didn't know I'm a big Yankees fan!)

Joe was part of my journey into the priesthood. His health saga prevented himself from being ordained. Yet he always sought out and encouraged other "men in black." For instance, Joe was a faithful member of Serra International and our local council. Serra encourages and supports vocations to the Catholic priesthood worldwide. My own journey, which I shared with Joe, goes back to October of 1941, when a 21-year-old Irish Catholic woman was working as a secretary in Reading, Pennsylvania. Her friend was dating a serviceman who was coming home and bringing a friend. They made it a double date—even though her father had told her never get involved with a serviceman or a non-Catholic. The friend was *both* a serviceman and a Methodist! After December 7, the men were recalled to their unit. In February 1942, following much correspondence, the Methodist showed up with a diamond ring and a Catholic catechism. Smart man! On May 30, he received Baptism, Penance, Eucharist, Confirmation, and Marriage—greater than a sacramental grand slam.

Sunday: The Sabbath as Pause

Two childless years later, the woman consulted her doctor, who told her that her chances of having children were 1 in 1000. She went to church, lit candles, said a novena, and gave birth to a girl. The doctor said that her chances of having a second child were 1 in 100,000. After more candles and novenas, she had a second daughter. Her chances of having any more children decreased to 1 in 1,000,000. You guessed it! More prayers and . . . well, I became one in a million! Joe loved my story.

He also appreciated my journey's Scriptural analogue with Elizabeth, the barren woman to whom God gives a miracle baby. That passage ends with "the people wondered what this child would be for the hand of God was upon him." In my experience of studying the Scriptures with Joe, he confirmed for me that we all have a story of miracles—large or small. Each person's birth depends on the chance meeting of quality people, the probability of sparks flying, coincidences and obstacles, also large or small. The hand of God is upon each of us always. Joe and I would share that Elizabeth and Zacharias probably died when John the Baptist was a child. He was raised by the community of Essenes, which apparently practiced Baptism. A series of public baths was found among the ruins. One of the occupations of the community was preserving and copying the Sacred Scriptures. Also, Essene was between the sea and the desert. Remember that John practiced his ministry in the desert, where people flocked to hear him speak. God clearly used this community to prepare John for his ministry.³

In a similar way, God used Joe's study of philosophy and the classics at Fordham University and Georgetown University for being a lay theologian. One time someone in awe of Joe's humble yet prodigious knowledge asked him, "How many graduate degrees did you earn?" Joe answered immediately, "None!"

When I first met Joe, I didn't plan on being a priest; in fact, nothing was further from my mind. As a child, I wanted to go to public school because they didn't get homework! I later learned the secret of *the best possible homework: Finished Homework!!*

My parents sent me to Catholic school. My dad drove me there on his way to work. This meant arriving at school an hour early. The school was locked, and in the winter, the only place to stay warm was the church. I was there a half hour before Mass with nothing to do. I noticed that the elderly folks who attended Mass would also come early. They prayed the Stations of the Cross and the rosary, so I started doing those things, just to fill the time. Of course, I always went to Communion. Some of you might remember the old days when the fast before Communion was three hours long. Kids who went to Mass and Communion got excused from part of the first class to go to the cafeteria for breakfast (because we had fasted). So as a young person, I quickly learned that practicing my faith had its "rewards."

Sunday: The Sabbath as Pause

In my senior year of high school, I dreamed of going to Philadelphia for college. I applied to La Salle and waited eagerly for the reply which never came. Reluctantly, I attended Allentown College of St. Francis de Sales. A friend persuaded me to participate in a community-building program. I figured it was a good way to meet a lot of girls. Instead, we met Father Joe Lang, who invited us to a college weekend retreat where I experienced the presence of God. I saw friends find peace and direction for their lives, and I wanted the same. I then found a spiritual director. After five years I decided to enter the seminary. This was the period of time when I met Joe. He was part of an important part of my picture for reflecting on life and seeing the ways that God directs each of us. We all receive the gifts of birth and direction, and we are always under His protection.

It's easy seeing why Joe ran great Bible studies with his wife. No doubt they had an ongoing marital conversation about Scripture—perhaps as in the *Song of Songs*, one of his favorite Bible books. Yet Joe saw all 73 books [of the Catholic Bible] [4] as one book. After all, *Bible* means "book" in Greek. Yet Joe saw the entire Bible more as a love letter from God to His people, from Yahweh to the Jews, His chosen, from Jesus to His Church. Joe was superb at getting people together and having everyone open their minds and hearts to what they heard. Whenever a priest or minister came to Sunday Scripture sharing at the Gossé home—and Joe was certainly ecumenical and interfaith in his formation of community—he became impatient when such "professionals" dominated the discussion. Joe almost always knew more about the Bible. His goal was that *everyone* would speak. Time and again he demonstrated that it's possible to draw out the truths of faith from timid or even uneducated souls.

Joe believed in "our native genius"—how God implants certain fundamental truths in our minds, which simple prompting will elicit.

It was especially neat when all sorts of people began commenting on a particular word or short phrase in the Gospel. Joe would open his Greek Bible and give us the original words and their Greek translations. While in high school and then college, Joe made it a point to learn both Greek and Latin. After all, in college he majored in both philosophy and the classics.

When Scripture sharing was over at the Gossé home, and it was time for hospitality, everyone "had their fill." Yet everyone was also "hungry and thirsty" for the next gathering. This was because Joe maintained a life-long understanding that the Scriptures are like an inexhaustible well of water. The more you would drink them in, the more thirst they are able to quench over time. You could never exhaust the deep well of Biblical truth.

A story of one of his innumerable surgeries underscored his great patience. The hospital botched an operation and created the need for more medical intervention. Yet he held no grudge. He simply grew in hopefulness for recovery. Joe therefore had much to teach me years later while I was undergoing chemo for my own bout with cancer. Joe was like the woman who suffered from a bleeding hemorrhage for twelve years (Luke 8:43–48). All that was needed for healing was closeness to Jesus in Word and Sacrament.

— *Father Larry Hess*

CHAPTER 2
MONDAY
A NEW WORKWEEK

The Spirituality of Work

Work was fundamental to Joe's identity. Without knowing Joe better and by not reading further, this statement might foster an image of someone married to his job. "Not so fast," Joe would advise. "Things are not always what you first think." A job is vastly different than work. Yet the two bear a relationship.

Joe's approach to beginning a new "workweek" centered on spirituality, on a relationship with a living God. That is why Joe's workweek actually began on Sunday—the Sabbath—marked by rest from our jobs. This statement is a paradox. Yet Joe relished life's seeming contradictions. Typically, when someone greets Monday morning, he or she thinks about a job, about tasks, about producing something, or buying or selling something else, or about offering skills in a labor market in exchange for wages. This is all sound thinking.

We begin the Monday workweek as artists, business people, craftspeople, laborers, office workers, in ministry, or as professionals—whether through a small business, corporation, government auspice, or religious institution. Some of us accept the noble work of raising children, caring for the sick or elderly, or of tending a household. Joe's performance on the job scene achieved excellence. Yet he always kept a focus on a larger picture. We are all workers in God's vineyard. God gives us an identity as human persons whose mission in life is that we work at revealing our identity. Our jobs and the "workweek" are but one aspect of our participation with God's work within each of us.[1]

Most people adopt a quiver of repeated phrases in life. We rely on such phrases for recurring situations. Usually they'll be in our native language. Joe not only reached in his treasure trove of English expressions, he gladly shared many significant ideas from Latin. One that applies to this chapter is carpe diem—*seize the day. In other words, make the most of every fleeting moment or 24 hours. For Joe, and everyone who came into his ever-widening friendship circle, or was influenced by his pen, seizing the day applies to every aspect of work, and rest from work, described here.*

According to Joe, work maintains a grounding in rest from work, whereby work and rest together find an entire whole of our being. This is why the Sabbath is the real beginning of the workweek. Sunday, for Christians, celebrates God's eternal rhythm of work, and rest from

Monday: A New Workweek

work, and the redemption of creation through the Resurrection of Christ Jesus. Joe fundamentally understood that work maintains an intimate and ever-present connection with faith.

Joe was savvy yet simple. Demonstrating a relationship between work and faith came to him with facility. He relied on certain building blocks for this relationship. One was his devotion to the work of prayer. In turn, prayer included lectio divina, *the work of praying the Scriptures. Prayer furthermore includes active participation at the Sunday liturgy—with liturgy literally meaning "work of the people." When a new workweek came around, Joe had already crossed a well-built bridge between Sunday and Monday.*

Work therefore encompassed Joe's vocation as a husband and step-father. He clearly demonstrated a real fatherhood to three children entrusted to him through his wedding vows. That's because Joe represented through word and action that there is no such thing as a step-marriage. A God-centered marriage between a man and woman shows the signs of fidelity, permanence, and openness to children. The mutual vows that sanctify such a marriage bear responsibilities and present a witness to Christ Jesus among us. Joe continually worked at being a loving husband and good father.

As Joe and Mary Clare's close friend, Deacon Dr. Bill Urbine, converses below about Joe's spirituality of work, readers will see that not only are family, job, and church within the vineyard of work, but so are friends, community, art, the imprisoned, and the poor.

— Ron Shegda

At heart Joe saw work as having a spiritual purpose. For him personally, he worked at realizing the Kingdom of God in the world. He accomplished this by representing Christ to the world in both his interactions with people and through his writing.

Joe approached work like most of us. He was very dutiful about pursuing an agenda of daily tasks. Yet most important for him was the time he spent with people. Joe was keenly interested in *being present* with people. I knew him in so many work capacities. Specifically, during the last ten years of his life, he earned a living as a financial planner. He became our family's advisor on money issues; he took seriously the responsibility of giving me, my wife Christine, and our growing family the best possible service. He especially impressed on me his commitment of giving us, as a couple, a clear financial roadmap for our retirement years. He was constantly encouraging me to make the right move.

In this regard, Joe saw a significant part of his work as being a mentor. During his everyday interactions with people—whether trying to sell us insurance or mutual funds, assisting me in my writing, or encouraging our family as Christians—we came to appreciate dearly and deeply the ways Joe was present as Christ is present.

Many of us view Jesus and the people around Him as constantly serious. Yet if we look closely at the Scriptures, we see humor. We realize Jesus enjoyed smiles and laughter. Joe was the same way. His witticisms, marked by an intensity for delivering his almost patented one-liners, seemed to come out of the blue. This showed everyone around him an outward display of interior work aimed at human *balance*. For instance, when talking about unequal pay between men and women, Joe was heard to say: "Did you know the prophet Elijah could have filed the first-ever sexual harassment suit against Queen Jezebel for firing him?"

Joe continually grew. At his 50th birthday party, he celebrated most that he was still growing as a person. This growth included an increasingly keen understanding of the spirituality of work. While unemployed after working for Congressman Don Ritter and before he became a financial planner with American Express, he saw there was still "work" to be done. *For Joe, being unemployed was itself an unpaid job.* Joe took seriously the job of finding a job.

Unemployment uncovered a brand new mission, involving work, writing, and encouragement. Joe's connections with the National Center for the Laity and ACTA Publications in Chicago fostered an invitation. Joe was asked to write the "Unemployed Workers" volume for the *Spirituality of Work* series.[2] He tackled this project with great enthusiasm. Fundamentally, he not only applied his personal experiences to a very hope-filled writing, he also contacted unemployment advocates and unemployed people all over the country. Joe became a one-stop, non-stop source of encouragement for anyone who was or knew someone experiencing joblessness. His motivation and conclusion was simply living out the Gospel. He saw advocacy for the unemployed as no different than his regular shifts at an ecumenical soup kitchen or in visiting the imprisoned. He listened to Jesus in his soul: "When I was unemployed, you helped me find a job."

> God is present in our families, among our co-workers, in the people we meet in support groups, and with all our fellow congregants. When Christians gather to worship, the hungers of every member of Christ's body are among the elements that are transformed into the Body and Blood of Christ. The unemployed offer their hungers—including their desire to work, their frustration at not being employed, and their eagerness to find jobs (*Unemployed Workers*, p. 38).³

During this period of unemployment, Joe wasn't afraid to do things seemingly menial. For instance, he would agree to certain short-term jobs where there was no apparent long-term payoff. His greatest legacy here was bringing the Scriptures to our local county prison. Ultimately, such jobs "paid off" because Joe touched people's lives and a lot of goodness occurred. I can't say enough how years after Joe's passing, people who knew him still conduct these Bible studies at Lehigh County Prison.

My most memorable experience of Joe's spirituality of work was as a young man. We were all members of the Children of Joy, a charismatic faith community. It was springtime, in the mid-1970s, maybe April, when my future wife and I had just purchased our marital home in South Allentown. I began living there. It needed a lot of work and cleaning up in preparation for our marriage. Joe was one of the few people who volunteered to come over and help. He wanted to wash the windows. Indeed, the day came and Joe cleaned a good number of windows. He was very genuine about doing a meticulous job. Yet more important than cleaning the windows, he enjoyed the time with us. Looking back, I can see this was Joe's way of celebrating our Sacrament of Marriage.

Work itself—the actual tasks of washing windows, being unemployed, or something else—was a way of bringing God's presence to the moment. Joe didn't make a special point of *talking* about religion or Jesus. Sure, he would do that. But Joe, with his wondrous face and discerning eyes, communicated the mystery of God by his very presence.

After knowing Joe 20 years, one way he approached periods of unemployment was writing about them. The contract he secured with the National Center for the Laity and ACTA Publications allowed him to apply the same "presence" he did while washing our windows two decades earlier. Joe was present with God to his moments of unemployment and to his "neighbor's." Joe worked at capturing the spirit of what it means to be unemployed. And he expressed that spirituality beautifully and movingly in words.

Joe's volume, *The Spirituality of Work: Unemployed Workers*, chronicles how unemployed people portray hope when their lives suddenly lose a daily routine of paid work. His conclusion was that, despite a threat against self-worth when losing a job, new, boundless horizons of meaning and purpose appear. Unemployed people mostly need a renewed spiritual approach with God, our neighbors, and ourselves.

Joe's insights about the spirituality of work, and his example of a written witness, have become part of my life. He taught that a spirituality of work includes embracing every day and ordinary circumstances. Work itself goes beyond our "job" duties because work encompasses the Holy Spirit's action in all dimensions of our lives. The Holy Spirit is the Person present within the Father's loving relationship with Jesus the Son of God. Regarding this Trinitarian relationship, Jesus says: "My Father is at work until now, and I am at work as well" (John 5:17).

Joe accordingly balanced a proclamation of the Gospel by deeds with a commitment to reading and speaking the Word. He did this in his home, at his

Monday: A New Workweek

parish church, and in the prisons. As Father Larry Hess writes in Chapter 1, Joe and Mary Clare hosted a weekly Scripture study in their home. Several people would read aloud the Sunday Gospel. Afterward, everyone would focus on one phrase or verse. Being the scholar he was, Joe sat poised for giving a Hebrew, Greek, or Latin meaning of certain Biblical words. Most important, his contributions empowered others to go home and open their Bibles with yet more family and friends—or to make some new friends while feasting on the Scriptures.

Regular Scripture sharing get-togethers in community were directly related to Joe's work as a lector. For Joe, parish membership meant preparing for and proclaiming the Hebrew Bible or Epistle Reading at Sunday Mass. Certainly, he was well aware that many people do not worship at a church—or as a church. Consider the imprisoned, for instance. Who was there to break open the Word for those jailed? It was Joe who decided to break into prison and share the Scriptures.

When Joe "broke into prison," he organized a weekly Bible study for the incarcerated in Lehigh County, Pennsylvania. Years after Joe passed away, a growing number of volunteers, many of whom he personally influenced, still go to this prison several times a week and conduct Bible studies. All during this kind of thankless work, where you never know the final result, Joe was persistent and gave people hope in their time of great difficulty. Of course, here was clearly an example of someone listening to Jesus' teaching that we should "visit prisoners."

You can see I've been describing a spirituality of work much beyond that of a job or business where we get paid money. Washing windows for friends, proclaiming the Word in church, or teaching a Bible study are equally valid types of "work." Foremost for Joe in non-job work was being a good spouse, a caring spouse, a loving spouse. As a step-father he further took seriously the role of nurturing three children entrusted through his wedding vows. For 25 years he showed each of them great love, and this was a great work. He inspired many husbands and fathers in their vocations. He still does.

Joe was very proud of his children as they moved toward adulthood. He acted on his keen interest in giving them direction and guidance. There was probably no greater a sign of this than Joe's interest in writing articles about spirituality centered on his children. He had an article published about each of them. Each of his writings draws forth Scriptural, human, and Christ-revealing insights about family relationships and personal growth. The work of parenting and step-parenting might seem thankless on a day-in/day-out basis. Yet Tim, Todd, and Roxine remain grateful in their adulthood for Joe's commitment.

Overall, a contemporary spirituality of work recognizes and extols excellence as a virtue. Joe was unassuming by his example of excellence. For instance, one year, without any self-proclaimed fanfare, Joe was recognized as the top salesperson within his financial-planning company. His accomplishment at the time was enormous. He was battling severe health obstacles—not only his kidney failure but also a fistula in his intestine that would not close. He'd have to feed himself intravenously in his car between business appointments. For over one year, the only thing doctors allowed him to eat was ice chips. Father Tom Orsaluk, in his "Fast Lunch" segment, verifies what I knew: that Joe would hook up his IV in the car and read the newspaper, pray, or immerse himself in the Scriptures.

Now, let's not forget that Joe did fall flat on his face with different projects. One of his vast writing efforts documented how he orchestrated having the incarcerated at Lehigh County Prison gain access to computers. Yet the attempt at publishing this work went nowhere. He confronted a similar result with his earlier written work, titled *Expectation*. In fact, while many of Joe's articles were published, many were also turned down. These experiences showed he was not afraid of trying new things or being rejected.

Whether he was employed or unemployed, Joe reflected core Gospel values. He strove for excellence. So when having a job, he would be recognized as a top performer. Yet equally during those times of unemployment, he took up the task of looking for a job as serious work. Concertedly, he would seek out other unemployed people and encourage them.

Joe was an unusual worker in his personality style. In some ways, those who knew, loved, and cared for Joe will witness how he could really get on your nerves. (Read Ed Delviscio's section in the next chapter closely.) Joe liked, almost demanded, precision. If you did not listen to a question or statement closely, evaded the topic of conversation, or engaged in some kind of prattle, Joe could show a biting and sardonic side of himself. Yet his joviality, good humor, and overall optimism were ultimately infectious.

For Joe, the ordinariness of work was something worth celebrating. In this regard he picked up on a theme in John Paul II's great Encyclical, *On Human Work (Laborem Exercens)*, from 1981. Emphasizing the ordinary, if not humdrum, was therefore another of Joe's contributions to a contemporary spirituality of work. Joe both lived and wrote about the ways in which God's presence pulsates within the ordinary tasks of any given day. For instance, he chose a job of financial planning for individuals and families. He made this choice in order to follow Jesus' teaching in Matthew 25 about the Kingdom of God and seeking a "return on investment." His Jesuit friends encouraged him that economics and finance were ripe fields for evangelization.

Painting and poetry were other expressions by which Joe captured God's presence in the ordinary.

Monday: A New Workweek

Now, Joe's interest in painting and poetry were not necessarily ordinary. We can see these facets of his life as more extra-ordinary: additional ordinariness! Like any good art, Joe's creative bent cast both a simple and a profound interpretation on life. Like the Gospel itself, his art presents many levels of meaning, from the ordinary to the extraordinary. In his 1989 volume of poetry and sketches, titled *Wellsprings*, Joe writes in the Introduction:

> Ordinary events and
> the people we know well
> can appear dry to us
> and dusty,
> like baked clay.
>
> The familiar can fail to draw us
> or offer what interests us.
>
> The following poems
> attempt to reflect on the ordinary
> dig a little and go beneath the surface.
>
> Springs of lively waters are allowed
> to rise up from under the earth
> and seep through the cracks
> of the everyday.

Joe's artistic expressions prompt that people first embrace then step beyond the ordinary, the routine, the mundane. By no means did he avoid the ordinary.

His example of washing windows demonstrates even decades later an appreciation of the ordinary. How many friends expect their friends to come over and spend hours washing windows? For Joe, this was an ordinary way of being Jesus, of laying down his life for his friends (John 15:13).

Getting back to his paintings, set on canvas with spare brush strokes, Joe was asked by his employer, American Express, to hang one on permanent display in a common hallway. He chose a work titled "Build." On the surface it was a work of art for inspiring his co-workers and clients with a deeper understanding of the ordinary work happening in the nearby cubicles. Yet while this work and accompanying poem might not be considered "religious," it certainly reflected God's presence in the world. Perhaps it was Joe's Jesuit roots that let us compare his verse with that of Gerard Manley Hopkins.

Joe's work was who he was. His work was not simply a job. Jobs without a spirituality of work end up burdensome, boring, and as instruments of materialism. Joe's vocation was as a Christian, husband, and father. He worked at proclaiming the Word of God in his parish and within the community. His written work branched out to the nation and to the entire world. Joe acted on the Word in the workplace. He also acted on the Word by writing.

— Deacon Dr. William F. Urbine

Midday Rest

Bang! When the Catholic Mass on Sunday (or any day!) concludes, the celebrant says: "Go in peace to love and serve the Lord." Joe clearly saw the relationship of Sunday and Monday. Go into the vineyard and serve! His keen wisdom knew that Monday's alarm clock began a new week of labor. We work to live. We don't live to work.

Joe accordingly understood that Sunday's deep reserve feeds Monday through Saturday. The Eucharist, Scripture, family time, friendship celebrations, rest, diversion, love's nurture—each of these carries into the workweek, if only we're awake and alert. You'll notice that all of the chapters after Sunday include some type of "Sabbath pause." In the section below, Joe recounts how he and his son Tim had lunch at home one day, and how this time together was part of a larger human and spiritual picture.

(Joe's essay was originally published in Living Prayer *by the Carmelite community in Barre, Vermont.)*

— Ron Shegda

My son Tim and I were discussing the winners and losers in the National Football League games of the day before. Each of us was home from work for lunch and was finishing up the collected dishes. From the scores and manner in which certain teams won, we started narrowing down who we felt would make the playoffs.

As we dried the dishes, we shifted into a lively, yet easy, conversation on local politics. We talked about zoning problems with a new mall under consideration and the work being done on a local highway. We noted an increased volume of traffic was expected. New industry would thereby come into that area.

Tim was twenty-five at the time with a degree in political science and a solid background in retail sales and marketing. He had developed an interest in politics and government. Tim already made contacts with individual staff members and legislators at the state level. His background in business provided him good standing for working as a public servant.

After we talked on some of these work possibilities, we found ourselves laughing about both the lighter items in the news and a recent comedy show on television. Our kitchen was soon clean and we both turned to the projects we had planned for the remainder of the day.

Pretty ordinary fare for the home and a relationship between father and son! True, but where is the spiritual life? How is a parent, in this case a father, exercising his role in the order of the spirit, as distinct from his physical, moral, or breadwinning capacities? The topics we discussed were pleasant and useful, but what did they have to do with God, Christ Jesus, and the Holy Spirit?

The *Song of Songs* is a love poem in Sacred Scripture. On the surface it's a poem or song about the love

Monday: A New Workweek

between a man and woman, a king and his bride. We also know this poem tells of the love that Christ has for the Church—or that Christ has for each person. The *Song* is filled with beautiful images and descriptions of all facets of love.

In Chapter One, the seventh verse contains a poignant question: "Tell me then, you whom my heart loves; Where will you lead your flock to graze, where will you rest it at noon?" This is a very gentle image, quiet and inactive, except for the grazing of the flock. It reflects the climate of love between two people.

From his early years of high school, Tim and I began sharing ordinary talks about sports, politics, humor, reading, or pop entertainment. I always considered these topics neutral in the sense that they were not a constant, personal challenge or some form of behavioral correction. These current events were something of a safety zone, a quiet area where there was no need for defenses by either of us.

In themselves, these conversations were not the ultimate in communication. The subject matter was not of vital importance; but that was the very point. Tim and I could relax together: rest from the various struggles of work or school or personal growth. We could really go aside and rest a while. That's what Jesus said to his intimates in Mark 6:30–32.

There once was a relatively brief period of a few months when our car situation was such that I had to drop Tim off at the local college on my way to work.

Our time in the car was brief, maybe fifteen minutes. The same easy style of exchange dominated these interludes. We could share our thoughts about his classes, teachers, and current news items. I remember no great, earth-shaking revelations on those trips. A certain sense of values and priorities would gradually surface as we treated our various subjects. Values of altruism emerged here and there, and it was always possible to reinforce the good theology or philosophy that was being taught at Tim's Catholic college.

Our drive-time manner was ordinary and there were no big lectures. A quietly growing foundation of love was laid against this background of rest and trust.

From the earliest time, Tim had been responsible about each of the duties in his state of life. He would take assignments seriously. He'd plan and accomplish his responsibilities with minimal assistance. When he was old enough for part-time work, he obtained employment at the local college and remained dutiful throughout high school and college entry. Tim quietly managed both his classes and, with some initial guidance from a friend, the grants and loans he needed.

It seems like an odd thing, but sometimes parents feel more as if they are doing *their duty* if they have struggles and challenges with their offspring. We can lose track of ease, rest, and love. At least parents know if a difficult child is around—making his or her presence felt—when things are not always comfortable or pleasant.

Good daughters and sons get lost in this shuffle. They go about their lives unobtrusively for the most part. They are good and obedient and can easily be taken for granted. Such children make life pleasant, and you might wonder what a good parent ought to do.

Good certainly does not mean trouble free or without blemish. We have only One without sin, and His mother. In our culture there are plenty of wrong paths worth avoiding. Yet basic goodness—filial piety to be exact—is an immense blessing and source of strength for a child. Tim was someone for whom steady, consistent nurturing would do the most good, in the deepest sense.

This was apparent to me on the academic level. When Tim began his courses in government at college, he was assigned some short papers. He was asked to write his reaction to a subject in one or two brief points. He would bring these papers to me before handing them to his professor. One possible way of correcting such work is taking a red pen and finding every mistake. Seeing Tim's effort and his thought in those papers, however, I was careful to note (in pencil) in a few places where he might make minor changes. I wanted growth in his confidence about his own work, and only offered minor direction signals for moving him closer to his goal of clear expression.

This process of correcting was very much in line with our entire approach to our mutual *general conversations*. There was always room to breathe, to move, to graze in relative peace. The trust and the growing love, witnessed in the ease of communication (as well as Tim's regular appearance on the Dean's List) were both background and goal.

This form of midday rest—sometimes taken in the morning or evening—seemed most appropriate for parenting our less troubled son. His academic success was consistent. His growth in the spirit of love was also consistent to the point where, at times, in his generosity and altruism, he risked being taken advantage of by persons less sensitive and considerate.

The *Song of Songs* expresses a mystical vision of love that has left the saints breathless. This *Song* yields image after image of the forms and structures of love that represent so many doorways into the love of union.

Our gentle and pleasant image of love, feeding, quiet, and rest is also a real door into one aspect of parental loving. We may not always be faced with great emotional turmoil in rearing children. We may find certain oases, at least for periods of time, with children who grow in wisdom and age and grace.

To this different type of challenge, we can respond by drawing from the waters of Sacred Scripture, especially the *Song*. The difficulty lies precisely in the call *to pause*, to cease from directing or pushing toward some inappropriate moment. In this image, love remains content *in waiting*, letting anxiety slide away and allowing the grazing of rest to abide in peace. Where is the spiritual life? The question returns now, no longer as challenge, but *as light*. These quiet talks between two persons, the gentleness of objective discourse, the lack of defensiveness, and the growing trust, begin in love, deepen love, and water love's growth.

We began with ordinary topics and ordinary situations. We almost took them for granted and then asked: "Where is God in all this?"

We have dug a little and found the buried treasure of Scripture lying just beneath the surface, glistening with promise. We do not have to go far or look beyond the very persons we greet in our daily lives. If we dig deep, we will find God there, and everything.

— *Joe Gossé*

Evening Study: Becoming Conversant with the Subject

Joe represented lifelong study. He always said it was hard work. Even when formal schooling is long over, we must dedicate ourselves to study. Study is a broad doorway for ongoing development of our mind, our character, our soul. Study lets us peer further into the mysteries of the universe, the Kingdom. Often if a friend would call Joe in the evening, he was not watching TV—that great pacifier for so many Americans. Don't get me wrong. He loved some TV shows, like Monday Night Football or Walker, Texas Ranger. Most evenings, however, he was engaged with a self-chosen course of study or some kind of writing project.

In this section, Tom Gossé recounts Joe's particular devotion to study from his younger days. Study is not merely some dry exercise. The object goes much beyond absorbing abstract ideas on dusty pages. For Joe, study meant a subject. It journeyed from the subject of a certain author or teacher to the subject of ourselves. Study is two-way. It is a conversation between teacher and student, between writer and reader.

Joe taught his friends about the difference between pedantry and educatio. (Yes, he was a student of the classics and therefore Latin; he loved to demonstrate his insights with the root meaning of words.) "Pedantry" implies instilling something into the one interested in learning. Unfortunately, pedantry might result in boredom: rote learning without much meaning. In modern techno language, we hear about "garbage in and garbage out" (GIGO). Not that something being taught or written has no inherent value. Rather, pedantry may not engage the learner and therefore miss the mark.

"Educatio," on the other hand, signifies drawing something out of the one desiring to learn. The root of true education, this style of learning is fully two-way. The learner him- or herself becomes a subject worthy of self-study. As Saint Augustine wrote, nothing pleases God more than a person fully alive. For Joe, becoming conversant with a given subject matter was a way of becoming fully human. Even more fundamental than *our jobs during the workweek is that we work on ourselves. Joe understood that being a good worker means that we know how to engage any given subject matter.*

He upheld a great corollary to education. Joe always endorsed the "native intelligence of the person." "Ron," he would say, "we must lead everyone to trust their own innate intellect, their ability to learn." The exception would be if the other person is a fool, or is prone to think, speak, or act foolishly—without correction. The Book of Proverbs warns pointedly in this matter. Another way Joe taught about coming to good and healthy and ultimately Godly decisions is simply by applying common sense—more and more lacking in contemporary culture. As Peter Maurin, co-founder of The Catholic Worker Movement with Dorothy Day similarly exuded, "We know more and more about less and less."

Joe promoted education in the tradition of Socrates: he asked great questions. He wasn't necessarily interested in the answer himself. But he knew you would be.

— Ron Shegda

When in tenth grade, I was given the task of writing an essay on justice. I struggled with this task because I was not, nor still am, a prolific writer. I did not find writing very interesting. I produced some "sophomoric crap" for Joe's editing. He told me to "try again." Furthermore, he told me that perfection is not the goal in a high school or college course of study. *Rather, the purpose of study is becoming conversant with the subject matter*. That was exactly what I needed to hear from him at that time. I re-wrote the essay and took first place in a city-wide (Bethlehem, Pennsylvania) contest for essay writing.

The thing I learned from Joey (and later my other siblings Jimmy and Peggy) was the perspective gained from a distance of time. It's very clear to me, more so than years ago, that they all cherished their little brother. With Joe as the oldest, they cherished the chance to teach me and share life's lessons from their own Olympus. In Joey's case, though, Olympus was benign and reachable—if you had the heart to climb further each day! That was the lesson, because being "conversant" meant reading, perusing, discussing, and critiquing the subject matter from many vantage points, and with many compatriots.

This is exactly what Joey did. He traveled within my reach, my circle of friends. He did this through my last year of high school and through most of my college career. He was peripatetic. Joe became a modern Dioginese, a searcher looking for an honest man, for a deep conversation, a friendly repast, time with the Lord. Joey was more than conversant with most subject matters when anyone spoke to him with earnest. He himself proved deeply involved in many subject matters from being so well read.

I was typically in awe and jealous of his careful reading of so many sacred tomes: William Lynch's *Images of Hope*, G. K. Chesterton's *Orthodoxy*, *The*

Cloud of Unknowing,[4] Romano Guardini's *The Lord*, the writings of Saint John of the Cross, and of course, God's own book, *The Holy Bible*. Many readers have much greater familiarity with these works than I do. Joe taught me that becoming conversant with such works meant reading, re-reading, and dawdling over certain sentences, phrases, images—or even over one word. He showed that study requires a real patience. In that way, we experience a saturation of the subject matter—a well-spring of living water.

He was also patient with me. We had a long-standing joke that he was my "permissive teacher." He allowed divergent talking and fooling around in his "classroom." This may have been to the undoing of his composure at times, yet it was always to my benefit as his "student." Later in life, Joe's legacy has led me to reconsider and re-read the wealth of subject matters he presented. *All of Joe's teaching reaffirms the cost of faith.*

> On my bed at night I sought him whom
>   my heart loves—
> I sought him but did not find him.
> I will rise then and go about the city;
>   in the streets and crossings I will seek
> Him whom my heart loves.
>   I sought him but did not find him.
>
> —Song of Songs 3:1–2

The deadly undulation of this mortal life is the greatest expression of freedom. I did not understand this when Joe told me because my understanding was only in a traditional sense. Joey's faith was always *love of God* and the openness of being loved by God first. Ultimately he was torn away from this life to be with our Father because God's love for him was so strongly reciprocated. The ultimate subject for Joe was objective love: God the Father, God the Son, and God the Holy Spirit.

— Tom Gossé

CHAPTER 3
TUESDAY
LISTENING

Listening to Clients

The great and devout Jewish philosopher, Martin Buber, wrote, "All life is meeting." Getting to know someone else, building a business relationship or friendship, enriches our lives. Conversation sums up our interpersonal relationships. We listen and we speak. Joe liked that order.

He excelled in dialogue because of his depth in prayer. God presents our foremost relationship. Prayer is listening and speaking—our conversation—with God. Joe exemplified listening first.

Joe translated his deeply honed conversational skills with God into a love of neighbor. For Joe, this was simply living out Jesus' Two Great Commandments, first found in the Torah. Joe knew how to extend his contemplative prayer with God to reading the Bible, to Sunday worship, to family communion, or to lunch with a business client—many of whom were friends.

Joe was just like the patriarch Abraham, a friend of God (see 2 Chronicles 20:7; Isaiah 41:8; James 2:23). That divine friendship was part of who Joe was when he entered into dialogue with another person. He knew that God Himself prays. God converses within the very glory of the Trinity. God's prayer is Jesus, the living Word, who returns to God as rain returns heavenward. The Holy Spirit, Who lives within all the faithful, is the conversation between God and Jesus. Through and with the Holy Spirit we can all listen to the Holy Trinity's dialogue.

Joe and Mary Clare's friend, Bishop Ron Gainer, lengthens this example of listening. Joe and then Father Gainer met after Mass at St. Paul's in Allentown. Joe and Mary Clare later asked Father Ron to celebrate their home wedding-anniversary Mass. Eventually an annual tradition at the Gossé home, Joe would one-day quip with his friend: "A bishop, a pope in his own diocese; a pastor, a bishop in his own parish."

I enjoy listening to talk radio. Some of these programs and hosts—especially sports shows—run contests. It forever amazes me how the host will give precise clues to the answer for winning a prize. You guessed it! The right answer is presented on the air, but the caller often doesn't listen. Joe had saintly patience that could rightly simmer over if you were conversing with him but confounded your ignorance by not listening.

Tuesday: Listening

Of course, one of Joe's most significant sayings is that "listening is our greatest expression of love." He brought his depth of spirit to the business practice of financial planning precisely because he concluded that the marketplace is hungry for the Gospel.

— *Ron Shegda*

"Listening is the greatest display of love." Joe taught this. First we must listen to God. Joe was a modern-day Saint Augustine who wrote in his *Confessions*, "I cannot know myself if I first do not know God."[1] Here we have the first of Jesus' Two Great Commandments: "Love God and then our neighbor as ourself" (Matthew 22:34–40). After a lengthy stint of unemployment, Joe decided in his forties to study and work as a financial advisor. Joe knew philosophy, theology, and welding, but not a lick about personal investments. He thought to himself: "This is a ripe profession for living the Gospel. Saving for a child's college education or for retirement is fundamental for most people's path in life." So he studied a few years, passed the necessary licensing exams, and took a job with American Express Financial Advisors.

Joe's famous story about a door-to-door salesperson emphasized his keen awareness for listening to all of his potential clients. As Joe would say *ad infinitum* to anyone who would themselves listen:

> There was a salesman who knocked on the door of a farmer. "Sir, I would like to show

you the best vacuum cleaner ever made." The farmer answered, "Sonny. I'm not interested." Yet the salesman persisted, believing the farmer was missing something very important for his home. "Sir, please let me demonstrate how great a vacuum I can sell you." "Sonny," the farmer emphasized, "I do not want a vacuum cleaner." Yet the salesman proceeded to take a small bag of dirt from his pocket and toss it onto the farmer's floor. "Sir, if this vacuum cleaner does not suck away every speck of dirt, I'll get on my hands and knees and take care of any mess left behind!" "Well, Sonny, you better get busy," retorted the farmer. "We don't have any electricity!"

Joe's well-trained ear, in the Prophet Isaiah's tradition (Isaiah 50:4–5), listened to everything his prospective clients said, including what they communicated non-verbally.

The Gospel led Joe to see that a family's finances are a precise way of giving flesh to God's grace. When Joe wasn't advising a client on his or her investments during the workweek, he was serving meals to hungry people at the Allentown Ecumenical Soup Kitchen on Saturdays. And he made sure about calling friends to join him.

As Ron Shegda has written elsewhere in this volume, Joe and I carried on conversations for years via voice mail. That's quite a twist to e-mailing or texting.

Tuesday: Listening

People today should find encouragement and validity in a willingness to have meaningful dialogue through voice mail—always picking up where the other person leaves off. Don't get me wrong. Joe and I would often meet face-to-face. We would exchange stimulating written articles. Sometimes Joe would give me a copy of something learned from the Jesuit weekly, *America*.

In the same way I reciprocated with Joe for encouraging his greater knowledge, it dawned on me that this learned man maintained numerous relationships where a focus was, not on information, but on inner-formation. We should help the other person's mind and soul to grow. Another way we maintained a studied conversation was by mailing such articles to each other.

This vignette is worthy of emulating. Joe and I began conversing about Father Romano Guardini's book, *The Lord*.[2] It's a great and significant book about our Christian faith. There was a noteworthy passage toward which Joe wanted to call my attention. So our parish secretary left me a written message on one of those older-style pink slips for when you're not in to receive a call—"While You Were Out." Joe left precise word on the point we were talking about concerning this book. He left word about the page I should turn to for what he was referring. To this day, that pink message note from Joe's call is still in between those pages of this book in my library.

— *Bishop Ronald W. Gainer*

Afternoon Work Break: Breaking into Prison

Semi-secular French philosopher, Jean-Jacques Rousseau, begins his famous treatise, The Social Contract, *by writing: "Man was born free, and he is everywhere in chains." In other words, humanity searches for our original roots: freedom—meaning, who would choose time in prison? The answer is Christians like Joe. This section could be re-titled "Breaking Open the Word."*

Joe understood the Word of Jesus: "You will know the truth, and the truth will set you free" (John 8:32). Whereas the average person might run from even the idea *of being in prison, Joe sought to bring the freedom of Jesus to incarcerated brothers and sisters. He jumped at the opportunity of "breaking into prison" for the sake of Christ Jesus.*

"For I was . . . in prison and you visited me" (Matthew 25:35–36). *When Joe learned of a prison ministry for the incarcerated in Lehigh County, Pennsylvania, he gave himself no choice. He wanted to serve. Joe willingly relinquished his hour lunch break every week for a Bible study with prisoners. Joe was like Jesus. He swam against the current. Joe broke into prison—for the sake of souls and the Kingdom of God.*

As Joe himself writes in Chapter 7's section, Inexhaustible Springs, *the Word of God echoed with resound in his heart and soul. Prison ministry is both a cutting and bleeding edge.* "Be mindful of prisoners as if *sharing their imprisonment, and of the ill-treated as of yourselves, for you are also in the body" (Hebrews 13:3).*

In 1989 Joe published a booklet of his poetry and drawings entitled Wellsprings*. One of his poems reflected on the arduous and lengthy task of finally obtaining computers for those imprisoned.*

— *Ron Shegda*

Prison Project—Putting in Computers
by Joe Gossé

Steps
    burnt on the bureaucratic coal-bed
        of hold buttons,
    trudged
        waged
            in the hard red clay
                of bureau referrals
        toward the forging
            of disparate links,
        computers to jail by computer commitments
            and regulations.

Did you ever see the movie *Escape from Alcatraz*, with Clint Eastwood? Or *The Shawshank Redemption*, with Tim Robbins? The whole idea of these movies is escaping from prison, seeking freedom. Who in their right mind would want to *break into prison for freedom?*

"For I was . . . in prison and you visited me" (Matthew 25:35–36). Jesus breaks into prisons to proclaim the Gospel. He breaks into the prisons of our hearts. Jesus inspired Joe to enter the prison ministry at the Lehigh County Jail in Allentown, Pennsylvania. Established by Sister Virginia Longcope, M.S.C., in 1989, various Christians would go to this jail every week to "break open the Word"—share the Good News of Jesus with those incarcerated.

In 1989 Father Harold Dagle was asked by the chaplain at the jail to start a Catholic program. There were many other religions vying to serve, but no Catholic ministries before that time. Father Dagle, from Immaculate Conception parish, gathered priests together to take turns saying Mass once a week. This proved fruitless because the people who attended had no idea of the sacredness nor meaning of the Mass.

Sister Virginia Longcope, M.S.C., had just come into town with the goal of starting both a prison ministry and homes for men who, when released from the jail, wished to continue a twelve-step program in order to maintain their sobriety. Father Dagle asked her to recruit persons to begin a prison ministry. Sister Longcope had a well-established record of serving the *anawim*,[3] the dispossessed. She had recently founded a halfway house for drug-addicted souls in neighboring Bethlehem, Pennsylvania—St. Stephen's Place.

Tuesday: Listening

Sister Virginia went around talking to various churches and managed to collect four volunteers. Joe Gossé became our leader.

If you ever saw *Escape from Alcatraz*, you'll remember the prisoner "Doc," who painted. Similar to Doc, Joe burst into the Lehigh County Jail with easels, canvases, paints, and brushes. His goal was to share the love of Christ through painting—while no one else knew what was going on!

Could Joe Gossé paint? We never knew. But he convinced the warden to allow him to conduct classes in painting with the inmates. He could and would always bring out the best in people as no one else could or would. These paintings were the result of his talent and his vision.[4]

To this day, the walls of the massive visiting room of the Lehigh County Jail don three 5 ft. by 5 ft. paintings created by the inmates. They change the atmosphere and mood of the entire room. The subject of the paintings is elaborate and intricate gardens, with winding paths in the brightest of colors: all signs of recompense and freedom by the human spirit.

Joe's presence made us imagine he was a representation of Jesus. Oh, that this could be said about any of us! It was simple to picture ourselves in the proximity of our Lord as he ministered to the downtrodden and lifted their spirits.

When Joe was on the scene, the focus of conversation was the Sunday Scriptures—shared in the

Common Lectionary by the Catholic Church and most Protestant churches. It is traditionally known that the Gospel writer, Saint Luke, was both a doctor and painter. Some historians attribute the *Black Madonna of Czestochowa*, a most famous icon of Jesus and Our Blessed Mother housed in Poland, to the artistic hand of Saint Luke. Joe ingeniously employed painting for pointing to the Gospel.

The Lehigh County Jail holds all sorts of people convicted of crimes from murder, to drug dealing, to non-payment of child support. Generally it is a "low-level" correctional facility. As Joe hints with his introductory poem to this section, America's prisons are a bureaucratic nightmare for those trying to visit the incarcerated—let alone for those jailed. "They really overdid security," relates Father John Grabish, "even though I would have my badge and clearance, I was often not allowed to enter and see the prisoners for the Bible study." Yet Jesus keeps knocking at the door of every soul.

There were clearly many conversions to the Faith through these Bible studies. "Oh, yeah!" says Father Grabish, after ten years of direct observation.

Joe Gossé had one standard: listen. His first and last teaching about love was "listen." Joe passed out copies of the Sunday Mass Readings and then went around the room listening to the men. Joe himself rarely spoke. When he did, you heard a soft-pitch voice which inspired everybody to turn their ear to him. One could not write a book on how to use Joe's methods for working in a prison. One had to see his technique in action: see the effect it had on the men and see how intently the men listened to Joe and Joe to the men. The whole scene was sacramental. No one could or would have that special effect on the inmates since then. Only if someone allowed Jesus to work through them as Joe did.

Joe gave us our standard for ministering: listen twice as much as you talk. We have two ears, yet one voice. Don't talk "at" the inmates; talk "with" them. We have used that standard for decades on end.

— *Diane Varra, Msgr. Juan Grabish, Fr. Juanito Gibbons, Malena Cecelia Gallardo Díaz, Ron Shegda*

Evening Work: Writing to Congress

How do we influence people? Our spouse, our kids, our neighbors, our pastor, elected officials? Joe knew how. "If you want to make an impact on someone, get to know the people around that person. They already have influence." So when Joe started lobbying our local Congressman, Dr. Don Ritter, concerning social programs—especially food relief programs in the U.S. and worldwide—it was very important that he got to personally know the people who answered Congressman Ritter's phone and who worked in his office.

Even though Joe was politically conservative, his very fiber witnessed that feeding the hungry is first and foremost <u>not</u> a political action. It's a Gospel action. Feeding those you know or don't know is one of the seven Corporal Works of Mercy. Joe understood that good Christians and good Americans should support governmental hunger relief programs. Of course he wanted to teach people about fishing and not simply dole out fish. Yet it's a scandal when people go to bed hungry in a world of plenty. Joe enlivened American culture as the most generous and charitable nation in the world. These virtues have deep roots in our Judeo-Christian heritage.

In this section, Ed Delviscio tells how Joe listened to the cry of the poor, the hungry. And he made an impact on national policy, however humble.

Ed's section also shows how Joe "worked" some evenings in a similar way that he worked during the day. Joe enlivened the pages of Scripture, including this verse from Ecclesiastes:

> In the morning sow your seed,
>   and at evening let not your hand be idle;
> For you know not which of the two will be successful,
>   or whether both alike will turn out well.
>   — *Ecclesiastes 11:6*

Joe lobbied Congress for the very purposes about which Ed writes. He had no intention of landing a new job. His virtuous labor bore unexpected fruit. As you'll

Tuesday: Listening

see in the next chapter, Joe "knew not whether his day or evening labors would be successful."

— Ron Shegda

Joe and I met around December 1970. I was finishing my senior year at then Allentown College of St. Francis de Sales (now DeSales University). Our contact was primarily at the capacity-filled noon Masses at Wills Hall. Although Joe was not enrolled at the college, he lived with his family in nearby Center Valley. He recently completed his studies at Georgetown University and was drawn to the vibrant Catholic community at Allentown College.

Eventually, young adults from Mass would hang for late-night bull sessions at the dorms. Joe hung out. It was hard to read Joe. Even then, there was something different about him. He was simultaneously *intense* about our many topics of conversation; yet, he also conveyed a quiet, peaceful demeanor. I knew little about the great health issues with which he was personally dealing—especially his manic depression.

Back in the 1970s, Allentown College gave birth to a charismatic prayer community that pulled in many people from nearby towns. Eventually we began meeting at St. Paul's Roman Catholic Church in Allentown on Tuesday nights. It's like yesterday that I remember Joe standing there at one of our prayer gatherings and giving a personal witness about his journey with Christ Jesus. His witness was both very honest and very painful. In the midst of his testimony, he read from the Scriptures in the original Greek. Joe did this because he wanted to be authentic. He wanted to give all of us the most accurate meaning of a Scriptural passage. Language and word use meant a lot to Joe. Back then Joe edified everyone listening about the importance of the Word, the Word of God.

In 1985, I joined an organization called Bread for the World, founded by Rev. Arthur Simon, brother of the late Senator Paul Simon from Illinois. BFW is a people's Christian lobby with some 45,000 members in the United States. As a sole mission, it lobbies the U.S. Congress for creating public policies that spawn economic justice for the unfed hungry at home and worldwide. Over several years I was coordinator for Pennsylvania's 15th Congressional District—the Lehigh Valley Chapter. Each month our modest group gathered at the First Presbyterian Church of Allentown. We planned and strategized for getting the word out on BFW to area churches and kindred groups. We focused on letter writing to our congressman and senators.

We figured a number of well-written letters would generate some kind of response. Now Joe had clearly invested his word and language skills in this letter campaign. His talent was finely honed, like a sharpened sword. Although he rarely attended our monthly meetings, Joe persistently contacted Congressman Ritter's office on behalf of Bread for the World. He wrote clear and concise letters to the congressman asking that he co-sponsor specific resolutions or bills

Tuesday: Listening

concerning hunger relief. It might be a resolution on hunger awareness or an aid bill for one of Africa's drought-stricken areas, or for America's inner cities or rural areas like Appalachia.

Joe would often relay that his letters and calls met rejection. This did not discourage him. Belief in a cause proved stronger than disappointment. Perhaps it was his Jesuit training. Joe would request a meeting with either the congressman or one of his policy advisors. He would ask, "Okay, what is it about my letter that makes you disagree?" Joe focused on the ingredients of words and sought the higher ground of mutual understanding.

Congressman Don Ritter was very bright. After all, he held a Doctorate of Science from MIT. He was also ideologically driven, entering office during the Reagan landslide years. At first he consistently voted against hunger relief programs. I myself concluded that the congressman adhered to a "trickle down" theory for helping people on the bottom economic rungs. Yet Joe persisted in engaging Don and his staff on the need for hunger legislation. Joe was unemployed in the midst of his congressional letter-writing flurry. However, Joe saw his letters as *unpaid work*. He labored at lobbying Congress because this was real work: part of his Christian journey on earth. For Joe, work meant walking closer with Christ and helping those around him.

With a moment of dazzling news for everyone, Congressman Ritter offered Joe a job in his Lehigh Valley office as a personal assistant. Joe gladly accepted. His early duties involved driving the congressman to and from the airport and to all of his local appointments. Don was shrewd. He greatly respected Joe's education and point of view, different than it was from his own. So he wanted to max out in regular conversations with Joe for the purpose of sharpening his policy and voting decisions in Washington. Joe's talent for keen listening and intelligent discourse later resulted in his being named a legislative aide.

Circling back to first meeting Joe, he was never an easy person to read. He struggled with many things: employment, mental health concerns, and relationships. For many of us, these kinds of multiple recurring obstacles might end up as debilitating roadblocks in life. Joe overcame. Years and years later, so many of us were heartened that Joe was fully employed, enjoyed sound mental health, and had a wonderful marriage. Joe was a saintly person. Then again, saints are of the next world. Joe traveled on the path of a future saint. He struggled with life's issues, yet his faith in Jesus and his Jesuit background carried him along. He was a person of many, many, many talents. As an essayist, poet, artist, businessman, and social activist, Joe's legacy needs embellishment from no one. His life should be inspiring to every person. He was in part a family man, a man of the people, and a mystic. His deeds and memory echo among many today.

— *Ed Delviscio*

CHAPTER 4
WEDNESDAY
A HARD MAN IS GOOD TO FIND

Driving the Congressman

Maybe it's only a casual smile or a twinkle in someone's eye, or a way about them, that initially attracts us to that person. Years later we realize we still haven't discovered the real person behind that smile. Then one day we see a beautiful soul in our midst. Their smile, their gleaming eye, was but a window to a soul where we never fully peered. Upon finally seeing into someone's beautiful soul, our lives are no longer the same.

In this section, Dr. Don Ritter reveals how getting to know a genuinely good person enriches our lives. We may have an acquaintance with someone—in Don's case he initially knew about Joe only from his letters and phone calls—yet we do not really know them. Chapter 5, "Thursday," witnesses the moment when Joe's son, Todd, *truly began to know his father. Here, Congressman Ritter develops a friendship with a beautiful person as they drive here and there.*

Jewish in his formation, Dr. Ritter reflects on Joe's sainthood. In Christian understanding, a saint is someone who allows Christ Jesus to shine brightly in his or her soul. Saints, always imperfect on earth, do the will of the Father. The Holy Spirit fills their inner being. When we get to know a beautiful person, we should ask: Am I seeing a glimpse of the Father, the Son, and the Holy Spirit?

After John Henry Newman was named a cardinal of the Roman Catholic Church by Leo XIII in 1879, his sister Jemima's grandson questioned his aged relative. "Which is greater, a cardinal or a saint?" queried the boy. Bent over, the churchman answered, "Cardinals belong to this world, and saints to heaven."[1] Sainthood is not something abstract or distant. When Christians pray the Creed, we acknowledge "the communion of saints." Sainthood, or its potential, surrounds us and is within us every day. We meet people like Joe Gossé in the most ordinary circumstances. Sometimes we recognize them when we comb our hair in the morning and plan our day—meaning our own potential saintliness.

Dr. Ritter served Pennsylvania's 15th Congressional District from 1979–1993. In the previous chapter, Ed Delviscio writes how Joe started working with Don. In 1986 Joe was hired as a special assistant, largely so the congressman could converse with Joe as he drove him

Wednesday: A Hard Man Is Good to Find

around the district. Don knew Joe had extraordinary things to convey based on all the letters and phone messages he received in previous years. In Joe's mind and heart, it was always ordinary conversation about ordinary topics. The congressman reveled in hearing a well-reasoned, opposing view about a given policy issue. Joe was so steeped in history and knew human nature so well that he often related stories like this about King Louis XIV of France—the Sun King.

Joe would tell how this king, who reigned for over 70 years, sometimes made decisions about governance. He sat one policy adviser on his left and another on the right. Then he asked both to thoroughly discuss the topic at hand. King Louie would listen to them as if following a tennis match. At the end of his advisers' conversation, the French monarch then formed his own opinion on how he would rule!

Joe later on became a speech writer and immigration support administrator for the congressman until 1990. They were a good match for one another. Each shared the quality of being rare and enjoying things well done.

— Ron Shegda

I've never met anyone quite like Joe Gossé and likely never again will. He was a unique human being.

As a political figure, one meets so many people who need something, want something, depend on you for help, or they want favors, your presence, whatever. It's something that goes with the territory that a politician must constantly give back to the people he represents, or he doesn't get his job done and won't be re-elected.

But Joe was different. Not only did he never ask anything for himself, he was the one who gave, gave, and then gave some more. He was a sweet, solid rock of emotional and psychological support for my family and me.

In the fast lane of political life where hyperactivity, stress, and excitement are constant, Joe Gossé was an island of peace. Coming home from Washington for the weekend, Joe would greet—not just meet—me at the airport. He would always smile, show a twinkle in his eye, and calmly lower my intensity level with some pleasant commentary in his soft and warm voice.

Joe was not just a driver for me; he was a close friend, confidant, spiritual advisor, and so much more that is not describable. Coming and going to event after event, Joe was there to listen to my commentary, feed back his thoughts and opinions ... and always to soothe and nourish my soul. He simply radiated calm and peace: indeed, love. Eyes twinkling, lips pursed in a smile, Joe was there to soothe and nourish my soul. He strengthened me inside.

Joe would delve deeply, with incredible ease, into issues of philosophy, morality, love, kindness, friendship, and loyalty. He knew what was really important in life, what could lead to inner peace and happiness. He had enormous knowledge but also the depth of focus to give impact to his knowledge. Joe was wonderfully *present* in our every conversation.

He would share his poetry with my wife, Edie, and me. We loved it and derived joy and understanding from what Joe wrote. His poetry represented his grand, yet simple, humanity. But at the same time, Joe wondrously delved deeply into the larger issues of life and being.

Was this man a saint?

I think of him often and miss his tenderness and kindness. If Emerson was correct when he wrote that "the three most important things in life are to be kind, to be kind and to be kind," then Joe Gossé was a prince amongst us because I believe that kindness to others was the driving force in his good life.

We spent a great deal of time together as I plied the Lehigh Valley as its congressman when Congress wasn't in session. Joe certainly was an important part of my life . . . and when I think about it, he still is.

I miss you, Joe.

— *Dr. Don Ritter*

Postscript. Joe wrote the following poem for Don and Edie's wedding anniversary. It was published in Joe's poetry volume entitled Wellsprings. *This poem is reminiscent of* The Holy Bible's Song of Songs—*a favorite of Joe's.*

Modern Odyssey

Genesis
   on a Delphic quest
      she, flaxen haired from a distance
         the labor of desire on an arduous climb
   he, able to envision
      the companion
for those distant, unseen reaches.

Land and sea
   geographies disparate as ideologies
      travels which widen vision
         and brilliantly clarified
            home —
      we will run together!

Corridors of power
         the stretch of binding union
   break point love
in the prophesied climb
   the distant, clear perception
      of companionship
   created amidst industry
      new business seeded.

         Love yields love
      and the climb produces
         fruit in due season.

Quiet Tenacity

If you knew Joe, it was nearly impossible to not realize he was always thinking. Someone could size him up and conclude, "This fellow is too demur. He doesn't have much to say."

Yet, still waters run deep. Joe's quietude was always preparing his great mind and vibrant heart for whomever he engaged in conversation. Father John Gibbons, who knew Joe for years and years, portrays two human qualities worthy for any of us. Namely, we will enrich this world and any soul we encounter if we act in meekness and with great courage. Joe exemplified such a quiet tenacity.

How appropriate that Father Gibbons portrays these dimensions of Joe—qualities endemic for anyone choosing the path of sainthood. Although Father John—an Irishman!—doesn't identify John Wayne and Maureen O'Hara's epic movie The Quiet Man, *this film portrays a certain cinematographic understanding of Joe: someone who sought simplicity in life, relished relationships with an economy of words, who knew his purpose in life. Trooper Sean Thornton from this movie challenged himself like Joe—to live life with a suffering love.*

Father John introduces readers to Jesuit author William Lynch, as do other chapters in this book. Joe initially knew Father Lynch for years only through his many books. Joe had so looked forward to one day meeting his intellectual mentor at Fordham University.

However, Joe experienced a lengthy shock when finally getting together. Everyone knows how it goes when we create mental images of someone before actually meeting—maybe only knowing that person's voice on the telephone or in looking forward to a blind date. In Joe's case with Father Lynch, Joe only knew his mentor from his writing—sans any photographs.

Joe felt a certain betrayal to his built-up image of his literary hero. "Ron, I felt so disappointed when I met Bill Lynch. He was a leprechaun, so diminutive in stature." Joe was expecting a giant frame that matched gigantic writing. Joe grew immensely from this experience. He learned that magnanimous faith, hope, and love have nothing to do with the bodily frame of the messenger. God the Father is omniscient, omnipresent, and omnipotent. Yet we humans have no idea what God looks like.

— Ron Shegda

"How's our big bad Johnny Gibbons!?"

His strong clear voice comes back again and again to the ear, the memory.

"Good, Joe. How are you?"

"Top form, Johnny, top form!"

Joe's response came from a man who just spent four-and-a-half hours in a dialysis chair. After years of taking lithium for bipolar health issues, Joe's kidneys finally failed. When he'd leave the dialysis center, Joe would strap on a plastic intravenous bag, get in his car, and drive to the next appointment.

Wednesday: A Hard Man Is Good to Find

This quiet tenacity brought him through another morning. While on the chair, he would make call after call to search for new business as a financial advisor. He set a company record for phone calls.

Replays of any day minimized his troubles. "Compared to the wards of the Wernersville State Hospital, it's a walk in the park, Johnny. Seven years, balled up in those back corners, until I was rediagnosed. Let's go grab some food, big John."

Life is a funny thing; the fact that I was doing business with Joe Gossé, investment counselor—with every credential—always struck me with whimsical humor. This was the same guy who used to make people very squirmy, back in those uncontrolled manic days, when he proclaimed the Readings at Sunday Mass in our home parish. Joe would deliver one agonizingly slow syllable after another. This was the guy who spent years and years in Jesuit formation, in and out of wards, or living with his brothers, sister, or wonderful parents. He taught welding at a local tech school. Joe wrote so many letters to his congressman that Dr. Ritter ultimately hired him to serve on his staff to research and develop stances on social justice issues. Joe then decided to become an investment counselor.

Joe was a humble Renaissance Man. He was more so a devoted Christian. It's easy for Christians not to know why they bear this title of grandeur and humility. Joe, like Mary, the mother of Jesus, knew every joy, sorrow, and glory of the Son of God. Joe was a Christian because he followed Christ Jesus. When we are baptized, we take on the Name of our Spouse: Christian.

As an investment counselor, he was responsible for a plethora of calls. Joe ignored the Gospel minimum of thirtyfold: he went right to the hundredfold! So came the phone calls. Then the messages. And more phone calls. I didn't know if this was another short business venture of Joe's, so I listened to him talk about the need for financial planning. And I listened, and listened, and listened. And the calls to me kept coming. Three years later I decided this *wasn't* some fluky phase of Joe's career and mission. So I figured it was time to sit down and talk.

The talk. Okay, market trends or hot stocks? Maybe a few minutes on those topics. But mostly Joe focused on leveraging his prison Bible study or on knowledge of his great Jesuit mentor, Father Bill Lynch.

Bill Lynch, a Jesuit, wrote *Images of Hope,* along with seven other books. Somehow all our luncheon meetings and Frisco Melts at restaurants would be melted into the Metaphysics of Hope. Jail ministry always focused "on the Word, the Word, the Word. Johnny. Keep them focused on the Word, on the page." This always rang true to me as a priest. Literary criticism of that day centered upon only the written word, while all other insights were seen as obtrusive to the words, how they reacted to each other on the page. "The Gospels can stand by themselves, Johnny. It's very rich. We don't need to intrude, nor do we need others in the group to take off on another idea. Let the Gospel stand by itself, Johnny."

This quiet tenacity continued, with follow-up phone calls, jail ministry reflections, and learning from Bill Lynch. Joe glided his clients right up onto the financial wave of the 1990s. These waves have come and gone, as Joe's life here on earth. But like the ebb and flow of the ocean waves, the Spirit's work never ends. That's just what quiet tenacity does.

— *Rev. John Gibbons*

Nighttime Entertainment: Walker, Texas Ranger

You have to laugh. Joe absolutely, positively loved the TV show Walker, Texas Ranger. *Outside of an inning of Phillies' baseball, a quarter of the Eagles, or Monday Night Football, Joe was generally never near a television. He had better things to do than watch TV. But if TV could advance the Kingdom of God, Joe was tuned in.*

With Walker, Texas Ranger, *starring Chuck Norris, there was something of the Superman ethos—or was it Hercules from Joe's classical education—that captured his imagination. Truth, justice, the American way: now that's a pretty good triumvirate of inspiration. If you called Joe during his favorite show, he'd let you know very quickly: "I'm busy and will call you back tomorrow!"*

Walker was no "wus" and neither was Joe. (A wus, in modern slang, is a person afraid to act or does not feel up to the task because of fear.) Walker and Joe stood for justice and kindness, yet with a toughness, a quiet tenacity. By this point in our text, readers know Joe was learned in the classics and Latin. One of his favorite expressions was "Illegitimi non carborundum"—Don't let the bastards wear you down. He was a realist in knowing that we all have detractors and enemies in this world. We all need to stand up for ourselves, for others, for what is right. In other words, avoid being a doormat!

Joe knew that television possessed an enormous spiritual impact, not only for the <u>content</u> of the program. He realized that watching TV was also a way for bringing distant souls into a closer communion. Joe would say, "We can create bridges or wedges." He innately saw how something as innocuous as watching TV could bring two people closer together. Watching TV, going to the store, or walking the family dog can create a bridge of growth for a relationship. The opposite happens when we speak with a mean spirit or act harmfully. These wedges break down relationships.

Joe published articles about each of his three children. The following meditation shows how Joe employed the boob tube as a way of better knowing and relating to his daughter Roxine.

(This essay originally appeared in Living Prayer, *a bimonthly journal no longer published by the Carmelite*

WEDNESDAY: A HARD MAN IS GOOD TO FIND

community of Barre, Vermont. Joe called this meditation Television and the Song.)

— *Ron Shegda*

"You are an enclosed garden, my sister . . .
an enclosed garden, a fountain sealed."
—Song of Songs 4:12

How can this beautiful image of an enclosed garden from the *Song of Songs* relate to the mundane world of television? For several years I have reflected on a rich connection between the two through the habit of watching TV with my daughter Roxine.

My initial recollection of the problem of television came as I attempted to talk about anything while Roxine was watching a program. The program, no matter which one—cartoon or mystery—had her glued to the set. In a real way she was enclosed or even sealed from discourse or conversation. Roxine did not want to be interrupted while she was watching or listening to a program; she did not want to be disturbed. Driving her away from the television or forcing her through sharp words to pay attention to others or myself was a possibility. Yet the words of Isaiah also came to mind. "Not crying out, not shouting, not making his voice heard in the street. A bruised reed he shall not break, and a smoldering wick he shall not quench . . ." (Isaiah 42:2-3).

Another path appeared before me. I decided to simply go into the living room and sit down for a while with Roxine. I watched whatever she was watching. At first these periods were relatively brief. There were other tasks in the home and other members of the family to spend time with in conversation. These brief periods of watching TV with Roxine were quiet moments of sharing and listening to what she enjoyed.

It was not a matter of insisting on making my way into this fragile area of enclosure. I allowed her this space and only waited for her to develop ease in responding to what we were both viewing. She was just entering her teen years. Laughter at a funny situation or comical gag was an entry into the garden comprising the personality of my daughter. We arrived at a place in our growing together where we found a number of the same things funny or humorous. The Three Stooges might have fallen into a cake, or some teenagers were in big trouble at home—a common plight for all teens.

Sharing laughter was equivalent to noticing a few green buds pushing their heads up through the moist earth. Roxine was less a sealed, enclosed and isolated individual, and more of a person responding to light and warmth. Behind the enclosure was a human being, like a garden ready to sprout and grow. This process of watching and listening, finding humor and the enjoyable, was a slow one. As with a garden, nothing could be or had to be done overnight. It seemed that the periods of watching could be brief, since there was a certain intensity to them. Presence was the key; waiting was necessary to foster relaxation and growth.

In time Roxine began to comment more openly on the various shows. The programs did not have to be humorous any longer. Serious shows evoked little remarks or questions as to what the plot was or why someone did something. At first these comments or quips were infrequent. Listening to them and following the program enabled me to give some response, which would meet the value of her comment. Initially, it seemed best to either reflect back what Roxine said or simply give some agreement to her observation. As she grew assured that her remarks were heard, she became more confident in observing or questioning. "The bruised reed" was not to be broken.

These remarks moved beyond laughter to different forms of compassion when a situation was difficult or sad. She and I could identify, at least in general, those events which called for a measure of sorrow or chagrin. We were communicating on a level of feeling and emotion that depended on common perceptions. Sharing a range of feelings in this manner was similar to digging in the rich earth of a garden. It was like turning over the soil and changing the clay to something more receptive to flowers and plants. The enclosure we started with was becoming more of a boundary around the limits and strivings of a young person.

The image of a sealed fountain, compatible with a beautiful garden, also rose to mind in these experiences of being together. Roxine, feeling freer to speak, began discussing what she actually saw on television. There were assigned programs from school and the news often related to her social studies class. Animal programs or the Discovery Channel would touch on her lab investigations where she had spoken with teachers and classmates.

This viewing provided easy links of communication. We could talk and exchange observations based on the common program before us. There was a neutral quality about these conversations—neither of us felt on the defensive. We were building an atmosphere of trust while some critical thinking was entering the picture. By this time, Roxine was no longer sealed or enclosed. If I came into the room when she was watching TV, I only had to stop a minute and she would engage me in conversation centered on the show. Roxine's lively interest became a delight! It was akin to seeing flowers come out in their different colors and shapes. Our talking together was now blooming into a real form of communion.

It became more and more apparent to me that television had a great value because it was something "out there" in front of both of us, which we could share. This developed patterns of thought which led Roxine to conclusions I often agreed with but had not uttered. She was thinking and developing independent opinions and personal values which she began expressing. She was also able to move back and forth from the play or drama on TV to real-life problems and difficulties she encountered each day. We used these TV programs to discuss solutions in her own life and then agreed or disagreed with each other. Again, this was a step-by-step process over a number of years. To me, there was great value here since her growth was not rushed. Instead I observed the sunlight of attention and the water of a listening ear.

It almost goes without saying that these years were not devoid of heartache, problems, and challenges—big and small. Viewing TV together did not eliminate problems. They were legion. What we had, however, was a kind of oasis in midst of the secular city. We did not have to travel as far as we could to engage something close. And the brevity of our random TV time removed any sense of the overbearing.

The Word of God once again emerged from the ordinary. In fact, the beginning of this story was when my daughter simply wanted to isolate herself. God's Word, like the bread that it truly is, can be broken and eaten. The fact of being enclosed and sealed came first in this experience. Sister—in this case daughter—formed a little bridge of warmth between the seal and the garden which was yet undeveloped. The entire process was not a matter of dissolving all boundaries between us but rather of respecting distinctness and encouraging latent human potential and beauty.

From the beginning, the Word of God is creative and brings forth life in its fullness. These words from the *Song* and from the prophet arose out of the circumstances and drew me back into the present situation and into a deepening relationship with my daughter. This became a living experience where each stage could be named and the named itself returned to us with power. The experience was overall a little one! It was a hidden thing and could easily have remained hidden. It required a small effort in digging, but this digging produced further reward. Attraction became the motivating force in a quiet, irresistible way.

We seek Him where He may be found. Yet His Presence is *everywhere*. Those ascetical elements of silence, listening, and deference—taken for granted in contemplative prayer—need not be limited to the chapel or the private room. In the midst of the ordinary, perhaps with a measure of sacrifice (I did not always like the cartoons or even the school related programs), we can come into the presence of God.

The same laws apply. We take off our shoes, recognize what might be strange, and listen carefully to hear those quiet stirrings or whispers. The least are always capable of identity with Our Lord. Scripture is one Song of Love testifying to that most intimate and hidden bond between the Son of God and those least, the little children.

— *Joe Gossé*

CHAPTER 5

THURSDAY

DEEPENING THE SPIRITUALITY OF WORK

The Work of Writing

Joe sought mentors throughout his life—in academia, business, and for marriage and family life. He especially knew the importance of spiritual mentors. These were his guides in this journey of life toward God. He often found mentors simply by reading their writing. Then he would make personal contact, by phone or in writing. Since he always considered himself a member of the Jesuit community, here was a rather ripe place for the many facets of guidance we all need.

He came across Jesuit Father William Lynch's books. Having established contact for some time, Joe went to meet Father Lynch in New York City. Suddenly, Joe's image of his writing hero was dashed. He was expecting a tall man with a commanding presence. Instead, he met someone diminutive and frail. Joe grew from this experience. It was likely much the same as when David's seven brothers learned Samuel would anoint their half-sized brother King of Israel instead of them.

The juxtaposition of a powerful writer with a small frame gave Joe greater appreciation of his favorite Father Lynch book, Images of Hope. A fellow Jesuit, Father Bill Dych, told Joe after Father Lynch had died: "Bill gave us theology, philosophy, psychology, and great ideas and insight about human nature. You have been the best person at implementing what he wrote about."

There was a humorous story when Father Lynch was on his deathbed (realizing even death has certain lighter dimensions). Maybe it was Father Lynch's Irish persona. A few people were by the dying priest's bedside. One of them said, "He wrote seven books!" Nodding in and out of delirium, Father Lynch lifted himself up and responded, "No. Eight!"

Joe valued the personalism of work and writing. Work should be something in which the worker feels personally engaged. Writing is a great example of this. Like any artistic expression, writing is a deeply personal experience. Joe told a story which illustrated the personalism of work—whether that work involved a vocation or avocation. He would tell of a man who owned an estate, employing caretakers for the grounds. Then Joe would say, "Ahhh. There was another man who had a smaller estate. He gardened his own property." Listening to Joe made you want to learn more about gardening,

Thursday: Deepening the Spirituality of Work

or at least about taking personal responsibility over the landscape of your life. That included not biting off more than you could chew.

Ernest Hemmingway left us a stark image about the art of writing. "There's nothing to writing. All you do is sit down at a typewriter and open a vein." (Be careful. Hemmingway blew out his brains to end his life. He was not in universal time!)

Joe's story also made me think of songwriter George Harrison. Here was a world-famous musician who, fundamentally, considered himself a gardener. The ex-Beatle lived with his family at Friar Park, Henley-on-Thames, but personally took care of the gardening. From what Joe was saying, it's easy to understand why George Harrison showed so much heart and soul in his music.

— Ron Shegda

When the historic 2016 blizzard Jonas blanketed the United States' East Coast, I was scheduled for my first Sunday as lector at St. Theresa parish, in Hellertown, Pennsylvania. A Reading that absorbed my preparation was about Ezra and Nehemiah.

Monsignor Schlert, soon to be bishop of the Diocese of Allentown, and I enjoyed both a greeting and parting exchange in the sacristy about lectoring—perhaps to the altar servers' edification. An elderly disabled friend of the parish witnessed later that Sunday on the telephone: "Ron, God will bless you for being a faithful reader of His Word."

Not thinking much of what this meant, as the Word of God invites, I reflected more that Sunday on the Reading about Ezra and Nehemiah. The next day I wrote an e-mail to Monsignor Schlert with only a subject line: "The Priest and the Layman." This was something Joe Gossé had taught me about these two Biblical companions. It's an appropriate phrase and depth of living that lay people have meaningful relationships with our pastors, ministers, or religious.

Monsignor responded by writing that there was no text. The text would be coming later; yet, I asked Monsignor if he knew Joe Gossé, my teacher, and this rich phrase. The response was simply, "I did!"

How remarkable that sometimes a few words can have great impact for a course of action and meaning. For instance, "I love you" changes the daily world of so many. Or consider how Mary, the Mother of Jesus, gave a one-word Latin version response to the Archangel Gabriel's invitation that she become the Mother of God. That Latin response is "Fiat." So be it. Consider that Mary's response, as translated into one Latin word, has immeasurably brought Christ and salvation to the entire world.

Monsignor's *two words* had an effect on me: *he did* know Joe. Reflecting on this a few days made me decide to bind a nearly completed copy of the manuscript written in memory of our mutual friend—*Conversations with Joe.* I would go to a Staples store about ten miles away the following week for a bound presentation after an upcoming Sunday Mass at our parish in Hellertown, Pennsylvania. Simple. I had the vision of seeing Monsignor after Mass, as usual, and offering him the bound manuscript, while pointing out the contents and contributors. These contributors included a very close, departed friend of St. Theresa's previous pastor—Monsignor Raymond Merman—also a popular departed priest of our diocese; a bishop who was once in residence at St. Theresa; a scholarly deacon; a parishioner; and everyone else.

It's interesting and most solemn that in *The Story of a Soul,* Theresa of Lisieux wrote that she devoted her Carmelite vocation in prayer for all Catholic priests.

When the day of errands came for trekking to Staples, I was told by the clerk that the binding procedure would take about ten minutes. So I disappeared into the store looking for a few other small items. *Returning to the copy center made me stop in awe.* At one of the copy machines stood the pastor of St. Theresa parish, one street from our home, who had replaced Monsignor Schlert a few years ago, but Monsignor still resided in the rectory. I asked the clerk if he would hand me the finished bound copy before paying for it. I then went ten steps toward the copy machine and greeted Father Tauber, whose back was toward me, by asking: "Father, do you believe in God?" He simply said, "Yes."

I then proceeded: "Father, this is unbelievable. I was intending to have this encounter with Monsignor Schlert on Sunday. Now here's the opportunity for a preview with you!!" Father then looked over all the familiar contributors of this manuscript in the contents. I told him, "If either one of us was delayed at one traffic light on our way here, we would not likely have met."

This was astounding. Yet our God is an awesome God. When I went to the counter to pay for the binding and another item, I asked the clerk if he witnessed what just happened. He was somewhat aloof. Then I asked, "Do you believe in God?" He gestured "so-so" with his right hand. Then he said, "That was quite a coincidence." I said, "Some Christians call these occasions a God-incidence. Carl Jung called it a synchronicity. We can all see it as grace: The community of Christ in the city."

Here's a 30-second proof that God is real. How can there be a building without a builder? How can there be a song or painting without a songwriter or artist? How can there be creation without a Creator?!?

This gave the opportunity to gently knock on the door of this clerk's faith. He said he was baptized, but wasn't sure of the church denomination. It doesn't matter. Nearly every Christian church recognizes the baptism of most other churches. I asked this young buck to consider reflecting on what just happened, and said I would pray for him by name.

Thursday: Deepening the Spirituality of Work

On the last Sunday before the 2016 Lenten season, when throats were blessed in memory of St. Blasé, I had the opportunity to present Monsignor Schlert the bound manuscript. Yet instead of outside a church door, as is usual, it was in the sacristy, because every parishioners' throat was blessed and they were no longer there. As the French say, "Voila!" As Yogi Berra or Bill Murray would say, "It's déjà vu all over again." You guessed it. *Monsignor Schlert and Father Tauber were both in the sacristy together after Mass as I presented the copy of Joe's manuscript.*

A new, important lesson from Joe was brought across to these holy priests of Christ Jesus. Not long before Joe passed into eternity, he said: "Ron, if you write a book, let it sit on the shelf for ten years. Then look at before getting it published." I had completed the majority of this manuscript ten years prior.

Wisdom on writing for the ages. The first Gospel (Saint Mark) was not published until 30 years after the Crucifixion.

A major lesson springs from the womb of this pregnant spiritual experience: Be aware of your surroundings, the purposes before you. *Carpe diem*—seize the day and the moment. We were introduced to this favorite Latin phrase by Joe in Chapter 2, "A New Workweek." Joe would let anyone under his influence know that if you were not practiced in seizing the day by later in the week, you could still start before the current week fell into history. He might add one of his famous "Ahhhems" for emphasis. He would advise that we "dig in." It's never too late. Remember that the constant and often new opportunities for "seizing something" apply to the vast rhythms of every week: work versus rest, job versus family, and the spiritual versus the secular.

A larger lesson follows, as Joe would aver, along with the progenitor of this quote, by Blessed John Henry Cardinal Newman: "I am Catholic because I believe in God."

The largest lesson is how a few words can have great impact: Fiat. I Do/I Did. I love You.

— *Ron Shegda*

Recreation as Re-creation

Not only would Joe leave you with a new insight, available for your personal adoption, he would give you the phrase or words for life-long memory and meaning. Joe developed a profound sense of relationship between work and rest. Work went beyond the confines of a "job" in "the marketplace." In Joe's mind, work equally applied to advancing our spiritual graces, such as joyfulness or humility, to writing a letter or article, or to a corporal work of mercy, such as service in a soup kitchen. In this regard Joe led a team of people every month for years on Saturday afternoons at an ecumenical soup kitchen in Allentown.

Thursday: Deepening the Spirituality of Work

Joe's daily and weekly balance of work and diversion from work emanated from a deep communion with God our Creator. He was steeped in the Scriptures. Of course, an understanding of Scripture begins with Genesis. In the first two chapters of Genesis, we witness God's creative power. Joe keenly patterned his life on God's rhythm of working six days then resting for one. Yet this was no sterile and boring equation. As we see in the Sunday section of this book, the rest of Sabbath can break forth into any pressure-filled workday when we learn how to pause, take a break, and truly rest our mind or body for a short while. For Joe, the key was always balancing work with some type of diversion.

Moreover, Jesus taught Joe how redemption brings renewal and re-creation into the creative plan of God. After an exhilarating and exhausting excursion of corporal and spiritual works (Mark 6:7–13), the Twelve hear Jesus' redeeming invitation: "Come by yourselves to an out-of-the-way place and rest a little" (Mark 6:31). Saint John Paul II the Great phrased the distinction between Genesis and the Gospel in terms of "the economy of creation" and "the economy of redemption." (See The Theology of Marriage & Celibacy.[1]*)*

In Joe's mind, opportunities for scattering needed breaks amidst work's flurries and furies abounded. For instance, he once wrote a related article for Family Magazine, *published by the Daughters of St. Paul. His article was titled "Supermarket Spirituality." The point? During the jostling and impatience of food* shopping—especially while waiting in a long line—we can come by ourselves with Jesus and pray, maybe even a decade of the rosary. When Joe handed another friend a copy of this article, Bob Campanella said, "Joe, only you would think of that!"

In the passage below, Rita Pursel recounts how a simple phrase by Joe changed her life. She and Joe knew each other from the Children of Joy. This charismatic prayer community formed at then Allentown College of St. Francis de Sales (now DeSales University) in the early 1970s. A few years later it migrated to St. Paul's parish in Allentown, where Rita met Joe.

— Ron Shegda

More important than learning things from Joe, we shared a friendship together. I always enjoyed talking with him. Yet there is something I remember *most*. That was the gift of one statement he made to me.

One day I was talking with Joe about being very tired. Several major activities were happening for me: I was in school, studying; I was also in training at the Jesuit Center in Wernersville, Pennsylvania; and there was a whole lot on my plate. So I told Joe about being exhausted on a regular basis.

Joe asked me, "Rita, do you need some recreation?"

"You better believe I need recreation," came my reply.

Then Joe astounded me. He simply inquired, "What do you think about cleaning your house?"

"What!" I exclaimed. "I'm so tired and you want me to clean my house? That's not recreation!!"

With profound candor, Joe said, "Oh, yes it is. Anything that gives you renewed life is re-creation *for you*. If you're working with your mind so much—taking college classes, then studying at the Jesuit Center—you need balance with something physical. That physical activity becomes your recreation. It will help you be re-created."

Joe passed along this very practical wisdom to me in the late 1980s, after knowing him about fifteen years. Since then I have looked at recreation so much differently. In all sincerity I can say that there are now times when I wash my windows and consider it recreation. The reason is that it gets me out of my head by doing something physical.

That's what Joe taught me. I suppose it would be the exact opposite for someone who worked with her hands, or maybe cleaned houses all day. She might find reading a book or magazine, or writing letters, as a needed doorway for re-creation.

Joe later detailed his idea to doing the dishes or vacuuming the carpets. He said these were great choices for study breaks. Jokingly, I told Joe he sounded like my husband, although my husband did not include the "re-creation" part.

Joe helped me see, not that my house was a mess—it wasn't—and not that housework was only a chore, but that I could quite easily refresh my mind in my own home. In this way, doing housework took on another meaning than as something else that had to be done. After all, when someone is tired, she doesn't want another thing to do, another job.

My sense of routine has since been transformed. I now know how to look around my immediate environment for a diversion from any source of tiredness. Joe helped me to have balance in my life by enjoying physical activities, such as housework, as something re-creative.

Last year during one of the retreats I led, I used Joe's wisdom about cleaning windows. Similar to *my* initial reaction, most of the women poignantly said, "You lost me!" The important insight was that cleaning *can be* re-creative *for me*. Everyone has to find his or her own sense of balance.

Many cleaning companies unabashedly adhere to the disclaimer, "We don't wash windows." In Joe's friendship and caring about me, doing windows was something remarkable. As I grew older as an adult, Joe taught me how to play. He was always someone I could talk to. He had words of wisdom. He was a master with his insight about the human person and people's spiritual lives. He was exceptional in his choice of words. Stated succinctly, Joe had tremendous insight.

Throughout the years, I noticed he could say the right words and bring someone back into balance. If someone was off-kilter from being overactive, or in an angry relationship, or whatever, he could see into this and say the right thing. What he said would help restore that person's balance. Yet almost as a living paradox, he was a man of few words. He could profoundly touch someone's life in a four or five minute conversation. He was very much like Jesus.

— *Rita Pursel*

Driving My Son from Practice

When it came to parenting, Joe acknowledged that kids do 100 things wrong every day. "What children need to hear about is the one thing they do right!" he would teach. Children need encouragement. This word means "give heart to."

Joe originally wrote this article about his son Todd for Living Prayer. *It appears here with permission.*

— *Ron Shegda*

That is why I am going to lure her and lead her out into the wilderness and speak to her heart.
—Hosea 2:16

When we make a practical application of this verse from Hosea, we may consider a favorite retreat house or the solitude of an empty church. Each of these applications is an appropriate response, but they do not exhaust the possibilities. There are many ordinary opportunities in which God lures us into contemplative activity. When we leave our home or office to pick up a child from a sports activity, our family car can be a form of desert.[2]

My son, Todd, has been active in organized sports for three years. It has fallen to me to pick him up and bring him home after practices and games. For two months I found this something of a chore. I had to curtail some of my office work to arrive at the field by 6:15 p.m. for the end of practice. I also changed my route home so I could accommodate our meeting. There is some irony in the translation of "I am going to lure her and lead her out" from the Greek. The verb in the Septuagint means, "I will drive her off her course." Changing my own routine to pick up my son was similar to entering a desert. I was leaving behind my ordinary pursuits and coming into the solitude of Todd and me. The "lure" was also present in this leading out, since I was responding to the natural love of a parent for a child.

Todd and I agreed to meet outside the locker room at the brown door each evening. When he got into the car, there were some starting points for conversation. He was always willing to comment about his baseball practice. I could ask him about specific areas, how he was swinging the bat or catching fly balls in the outfield. The interest we shared in baseball gave us something we could discuss. Sports are a fairly neutral topic because they are basically play, exercise, and a measure of fun. This makes them an ideal starting point for a daily conversation. We talked about Todd's hits of the day as well as the improved hitting of other team members. An exceptional catch would always be a topic.

Chatting about sports with a young child sounds like a far cry from Hosea and the wilderness. But wilderness is a desert, a deserted place. The main thing Yahweh wants us to leave behind in meeting with Him is our own concerns and plans. The wilderness signifies that place where we effectively shed our baggage of thoughts about ourselves. In order to be present with Todd, I actually had to let go of my business and pay attention to those activities where he was immediately involved. I had to lose myself for another. The wilderness was the family car and the brown door.

Even the discipline of turning to a topic like sports, with its relevance to this child, was an exercise in my ability to turn aside and rest a while. Simple practice like this in the play of give and take is remote preparation for turning toward God's own rest and play.

Our trip home was usually short—fifteen or twenty minutes. Because of the development of a child of twelve or thirteen, a longer time might have been taxing. The short time limited the number of points we could cover and enabled us to save topics for another day. This way we usually had something to look forward to from day to day. Of course, it took a number of rides to develop this much interest. In the beginning I would ask Todd how his day was and wait for an answer. At first his answers were short, one or two syllables. But, as he further appreciated my interest in his practices, he began describing his base running or a good double play by three teammates. A home run was great cause for joy, especially one he hit over the shed in center field.

"[I will] speak to her heart." The word "speak" used in this phrase can also mean *chatter*. This is precisely what Todd and I were doing as we drove home from his practice. We were conversing easily with one another. It is for this very reason that Yahweh leads us out and into the wilderness. This ease in talking or chatting with one another is founded on trust and receptivity. Communion between father and son parallels and nourishes the communion sought in contemplation of God. The structures of both are identical.

In the context of this ease, the focus on one topic at a time fits with the freedom to dwell on one word or phrase coming from the mouth of God. The clutter of many thoughts and considerations gradually slides away in the scarcity of this type of desert. One topic shared in mutual interest and relish yields much fruit in both human and Divine conversation.

Attention to sports between Todd and me developed a mutual interest that began spilling over into other areas. Since Todd played sports with his classmates, there was an easy bridge to school and his academic work. Beginning with sports helped remove much of the defensiveness that can enter discussions of schoolwork between a father and son. Now we could move into a more serious subject and surround it with our friendliness. Yahweh is able to lure us into deeper solitude through the friendliness we develop in our communication. Mutuality grows and expands into wider fields of interest.

With Todd, I would draw analogies between sports and school. It's easy to show how sports require organization, knowledge, and teamwork—all ingredients of good academic behavior and general conduct. In baseball, organization is crucial if a double play or a relay from the outfield are going to work. I could therefore help Todd see the importance of arranging numbers in the right order for a math problem to work. Only when a team takes direction from the coach will they play well. In a classroom, students enjoy their work if they cooperate with the teacher and do not pull against her or him.

These parallels drawn from sports enabled us to look at similar goals rather than my pointing a finger at Todd for not achieving in specific subjects. Just as he wished to improve on the field, he developed interest of improving in school. His enthusiasm for sports gradually became linked with enthusiasm for studies and constructive behavior in school. This entire development was a process that took a few years and is still proceeding.

Yahweh lures us and leads us into the wilderness, the strange and the uncomfortable, in much the same way. We begin our attraction to God by dwelling on verses such as "Yahweh is my shepherd, I shall not want," or, "Ask and you shall receive." We delight in the fact of God's love for us and in His willingness to hear our petitions. We are very happy, and rightly so, to experience a God who cares for our concerns and interests. God's responsibility for our welfare, His shepherding, speaks to our hearts.

God's love continues to lead us out of our own circle of interest into the hitherto unknown areas of Christian work. We begin to look at enemies in a new way—as unknown people, different but possible friends. Another wilderness area could be all those little ones whom we easily overlook and neglect to listen to or feed. The social outcasts, the very poor, the prisoners, come gradually into focus.

The movement in both these conversations is the same. Easy talking with the other (Other), staying on a common ground of interest, enables the process of being lead out to the new, the strange, and the uncomfortable. In the wilderness of the new task or challenge, knowledge of a loving communion and the already established common bonds of mutual interest gradually transform the desert into an oasis. Yahweh, my Friend, is there and we are continuing to talk. Our communion changes my outlook.

Finally, I used to kindle interest with Todd through the choice of certain anecdotes from my own day. When we first started our conversations, the interjections about my experiences had to be very brief.

Thursday: Deepening the Spirituality of Work

Todd was interested in sports or an event at school and wanted to get back to those topics as quickly as possible. I would mention talks I gave to high school students or at other area schools. Sometimes I even visited a counselor at Todd's school. At the time I worked at a trade school and traveled to different high schools for recruiting students. Todd might ask a question or make a comment about my experience. *One day he got into the car and asked me about my day.* I knew we were turning a corner.

My questions about Todd's baseball practices and his work in school did two things: they actively demonstrated my interest in Todd and provided him with a pattern for responding to me. He could ask where a school was located or if any baseball or football players had come to talk to me about learning a trade. Then Todd began asking about aspects of the welding trade. My interest in Todd and his activities developed in him a capacity for interest in some of my work and concerns. Two-way conversation became a reality.

Yahweh lures and leads us out into the wilderness in order to talk with us. He begins by speaking to our concerns, but gradually He leads us out to concerns and areas that are strange and different. What often begins as more of a chore turns, little by little, into the mutual interest of friends who really care for one another and for the concerns they willingly share. A river runs through the desert.

— Joe Gossé

CHAPTER 6
FRIDAY
LONG DAYS, HARD NIGHTS

Deeper Conversations: Universal Time

In working with Tom Gossé on this book, it seemed like Joe got mixed-up in our conversations. He was certainly tuned-in through prayer. For starters, with Tom in Texas and me in Pennsylvania, much of our dialogue—in exact parallel with Joe—was carried on by voice mail. And it was hysterical, full of Joe-isms.

For instance, with Joe, Tom, and I all being Anglophiles, I appreciated Tom's lengthy voice mail greeting recorded in an English accent. One of my messages to Tom was left for G. K. Chesterton, saying it was Hilaire Belloc. Just like Joe, Tom's return message in part corrected me by saying, "It's Hill-AIR, not HILL-ary." I shot back, with both of us still speaking by voice mail, that this is hilarious! Moreover, I was able to give Tom a few zingers.

An earlier voice mail by Tom complained he did not know what to do with a partial typescript sent his way. Tom was burdened with a lengthy search for my phone number, perhaps challenged by caller ID or transcribing good voice mail notes. My reply voice mail was that if he read and kept my cover letter (head), he would have my number and know exactly the next step toward publication!!! "Oh," Tom continued during our digital dialogue. "I found your letter buried in the large envelope of draft pages."

Joe would never let such an opportunity slip away. Nor did I. "God save the Queen," I said as our voice mail repartee continued. "We 'ave a writer 'ere who doesn't know 'ow to read! We 'ave a reader from Texas who can't sort out mail from the pony express!!!"

During this banter, Tom commented I had too many Ronald Reagan stamps on my package. "While Joe would approve, that's too many stamps for me," Tom barbed by voice mail from Texas. He later followed this sub-thread of conversation by cross-referencing it with a comment about "a skip between conservatism and liberalism in the Church." With a perfect Joe-like riposte, I answered: "Tom, in the Church, there is no right or left, there's only right!" Joe smiled in heaven.

In seriousness, the proper terms for framing "governance" in the Church are not liberalism and conservatism. The right framework is "orthodoxy" and "unorthodoxy"—meaning true belief and divergent belief. (The Eastern Churches give special accent to orthodoxy.)

The Magisterium, or teaching authority of the Church, must be and always is orthodox by command of Christ through the Holy Spirit. God the Father ordains it so.

We could also contrast orthodoxy with heresy— error in teaching about the faith. The breaking point with orthodoxy is schism—rejection of true faith. This is why Orthodoxy, *the compelling classic by G. K. Chesterton, was a staple in Joe's library.*

Secondly from this section's introduction, let's go back to Joe being part of the conversation between Tom and me. Tom pointed out squarely, "Ronnie, I have become Joe." "Well," I said. "Joe was a rare bird who would sometimes call me by my boyhood name. Joe was both rare yet did things well-done at the same time." Tom and I recognized that our standard of conversation together was Joe.

In fact, I coined an acronym for our North-South phone tag: WWJS: What Would Joe Say? To me—and perhaps for every contributor between these covers— this is the stuff of saints. Saints are people, confirmed by the Church after death, who allowed the Light of Christ to brightly shine in their souls. They were people among us like Mary, the Mother of God, who said "Yes! Fiat!" to Jesus. So when we in turn reflect on those who clearly become saints in the world to come, we really see Christ.

It was appropriate that Tom and I would share Joe as a measure of our friendship and conversation. Our relationship multiplied from twofold, to threefold, to fourfold: Tom and me, then also to Joe and Jesus. Tom phrased our developing conversation another way: "Ron, everyone between these book covers is channeling Joe!"

As Tom introduces how his brother discovered the reality of "universal time," he traces Joe's initial awareness of what this means. As Joe ministered to the black community in Washington, D.C., he kept hearing grandmothers use the term "right on time." This puzzled both Joe and then Tom. But it's easy to understand its double meaning. First, when we or someone else arrive when we're supposed to, we or they are "right on time." OK. We do what we're supposed to; we have integrity.

Yet the second meaning is more hidden and profound. There are occurrences of grace in our lives where we recognize God's presence. Life's transpirations are rightly, on time. There's a rightness to what is happening that only God could orchestrate.

One final introduction to universal time is a Gospel phrase Saint John Paul II the Great applied to the New Evangelization: "Go out into the deep" (Luke 5:4–11). In other words, Jesus and His Vicar of Christ are saying: "Go further into the depth of your faith." This is what precisely occurs when the timelessness of the Gospel transfixes us into universal time.

— Ron Shegda

Friday: Long Days, Hard Nights

Letters to My Brother Joe in Universal Time

May 12, 2018: Letter #1—To my brother Joe in Universal Time

Dear Joey,

This is a little *crazy*—I know you get my meaning—writing these letters to you 17-plus years after your death. I especially miss those last few months with you when we'd chat and discuss the future. But you were with Jim and Mary and that was better and more appropriate, more necessary for them, for our brother Jim in particular. I hope you gave him a sense of belonging and peace that he couldn't seem to get on his own. Yes, I was working hard in those months and those years before, trying to prove to myself that I was good enough to be a Gossé, a son of Joe and Peg, youngest of the family, brother of Joe, Jim, and Peggy! I can't tell yet whether or not that paid off. I will have to await the outcome of *universal time*.

Joe often spoke about universal time. It's a dimension of "measurement" different from clocks, the earth's rotation, or the linear progression of time. Fundamentally, universal time for humanity is *spiritual—by and of God*. One of Joe's favorite authors, fellow Jesuit Pierre Teilhard de Chardin, evoked what Joe and many understand by this reality.[1] You can call it "the big picture." This happens when we step away from moment-by-moment experiences and realize something meaningful has transpired for all time.

Joe first heard about "universal time" while ministering among poor black neighborhoods in Washington, D.C. He would often hear elders in the community speak about something unexpected or remarkable that took place in the routines of their day. They would say, "That happened in *universal time!*" It would be something meaningful worth repeating far into the future. Something bearing a dimension of the miraculous. In other words, a clear sense of God's presence—having been touched by God's mysteriousness yet without knowing the right words for a description.

Quite a few years ago I was charged with picking you up from an appointment or from somewhere Pop told me about. I showed up late; I arrived in *linear time*, but you told me that I was "right on time, right on *universal time* . . ." You had found a fruitful way to spend the difference between when I was supposed to show up and when I finally arrived. You were unraveling the space between linear time (an artificial metric of change), emotional control, the action of living, and with the spiritual life. You were living in universal time, a place that allowed (and allows) us to encounter the Spirit. I started studying a little bit of your friend *Teilhard.* And as I read, then re-read, then reflected on his writing about "living" in *The Divine Milieu,* I started understanding universal time.

It strikes me that universal time is not event driven, yet it produces and procures room for meaningful eventuality. Such as the time when you were waiting for me and you encountered people, while you were waiting, who shared with you what they were living and opened you for an encounter with the Holy Spirit. You did not use the time in anxious pacing or furious emotion, instead you "wasted" the clock time in conversation with strangers, who became personal to you. You had worked yourself through the disappointment and resentment, the frustration of that over which you had no control, and broke through to something over which you had complete control. As Teilhard would write, "You both attached and detached, in a moment of divine milieu with Christ."

I distinctly remember you telling me the story of being placed in a straitjacket one time at Sibley or St. Elizabeth's in Washington, D.C. You experienced an "episode" of manic depression. Within the confines of the straitjacket you could only express your frustration by kicking the padded wall of the room. You said that you kicked that wall so hard at first, expressing your fury at being totally restrained, and as that fury gradually drained your energy, you kicked less and less. You then retreated to the interior of your soul, seeking quietude.

I was able to picture you in the straitjacket; I was frustrated just from the image itself. I also envisioned you kicking the wall and could see the people around you watching strictly from the outside. In my vision they did not lift a finger to help you. I placed myself into your mental straitjacket. I felt scared, angry, and frustrated for you. On the other hand, you managed to move yourself from linear time and travel into universal time—God's time. You worked at turning that event around and got more from it, something greater than external restraint from a supposed greater harm. You changed your temporary imprisonment into a search for inner freedom. As I recall our continuing conversation about that period, you began studying Saint Augustine's insights about *freedom to* as opposed to the more secular *freedom from.* Freedom to explore creation with God became your guide. You discovered "freedom to" express the full fury and anxiety of your manic state without the painful consequences of hurting others or yourself.

Within the expression of universal time there resides God's expression of living this life with the tools of love, hope, and faith, tools that are much more difficult to use than within the hellish crush of linear time.

May 12, 2018: Letter #2—To my brother Joe in Universal Time

Dear Joe,

Continuing our conversation with us and our readers in universal time, I would like to share a story that you may have already heard or been present for within the *realm* of the Kingdom of Heaven. I believe the divine milieu or Presence *is* the Kingdom of Heaven, and it is my constant prayer that our entire reunited family—you, Jim, Dad, Mother, Mom Mom, Aunt Nelly, et al—are together in relationship to this earth within His Presence, sharing His Family, experiencing new life! Within this context it is my belief that our time here in this multiversity is also a shared experience, but within the meaning and reality of the Divine.

In the fall of 2008 we took your nephew, Thomas, up to DeSales University—in our old 'hood of Center Valley, Pennsylvania—from Houston to start college. It was with Jean, Charlie, and myself. We stopped by Tara and Jason's place in the country at Huffs Church, a village in Berks County, Pennsylvania, and visited with them. We parked our RV nearby in Macungie so that we could get Thomas set up for four years of campus life. Some parts of this transition were very smooth and some were really rough. (I submit this is a common universal time for any family packing up a collegian for his or her new adventure in life.) Thomas was preparing himself for this BIG transition to life on his own: away from his high school friends; away from his home and bedroom, where he had constructed a sort of security; and away from his brother Charlie, his closest companion, co-conspirator, friend, and antagonist. I found out later how much anxiety this caused Thomas and how he dealt with this going forward.

Painful times we experience closer up than further away shake our souls the most. The close-up perspective is the most difficult. We tend to experience nearby pain alone, despite compatriots alongside. Our reality of a painful experience invites us to either seek the meaning, or to turn away. I believe the search for meaning within the pain of our experiences brings us to universal time and within the presence of God. He seeks us inside our pain, our questioning, our anxiety—and we have the opportunity to reach out to Him as Abba, Daddy. Or we reject that route and ultimately choose a way with less succor and more pain and discomfort.

We delivered Thomas to the campus on the appointed day and met his new roommate. We got him set up. The rest of our family got ready for our return trip to Texas. A very painful "elephant appeared in his dorm room" as we needed to leave so he could begin university life. We had to say goodbye, for now, BUT also FOREVER in a way. This was a more permanent transition, yet one which we could still revisit for a while within this world.

We left the DeSales campus and headed back to the RV campground, namely Jean, Charlie, and myself. The car was quiet after a few rounds of small talk concerning the dorm, Josh, Thomas' new roommate, and some discussion of how well Thomas would adjust to this new life and his studies. (As an aside, Thomas majored in philosophy for four years, something of which I am very proud and happy for him.) The route we took back to the campground coincidentally (cf. UNIVERSAL TIME) took us through your old Allentown neighborhood, Joey. We had to stop for allergy medicine for

Friday: Long Days, Hard Nights

Charlie at the Giant grocery store in the Village West Shopping Center off Tilghman Street. Whenever he would come back to Pennsylvania for a visit in the summer, the flora would give him fits, which he did not experience in Texas.

By the time we got to the Giant, there was a pall hanging over the interior of the car. It was a combination of saying goodbye to Thomas for the first time in his life, driving through your old neighborhood, without you there, and preparing for a new phase of living with Charlie, Jean, and me. This miasma was very heavy, palpable, and physical, which no amount of air-conditioning or open windows could seem to displace or move. Jean and Charlie were going back and forth about something when I parked the car and went into the Giant to get the antihistamine for Charlie.

I got out and went into the store, searching for the medicine. I proceeded directly to pay for it. A woman with a young child was in front of me checking out. She couldn't pay for her whole order, so she started removing things from her cart. I wanted to get out of the store and return to the RV, physically and emotionally drained from our day. I looked forward to "decompressing" in my own space before we hit the road back to Texas. I offered to pay for the items this lady needed, hoping to get on with check out. We got that straightened out. As I moved up to the cashier, I noticed a woman whose face I remembered from the days of the St. Paul's charismatic prayer group in

Allentown that you introduced me too when I was in high school. I think her name was Kate Brown, but my memory for names has never been great, whereas faces are my strong suit. I said hello to her and told her who I was. When I did, she said: "You're Joe Gossé's son?" I replied, "Yes, and Joey Gossè's brother." She further marveled, "How is Joe? I haven't seen him in ages?" Sadly my response was, "Joey's dead, he died in September 2000." She was shocked and dismayed that you had passed away. Yet you sparked happy memories and we continued to reminisce about St. Paul's, you, our families, and our lives since those *heady days* in the early 1970s, when that prayer group was active and growing and moving with the Holy Spirit. It was, to say the least, an interesting encounter *but not nearly as interesting* as what would happen next!

We said our goodbyes and I took the medicine and my own thoughts back to the car. When I returned and opened the door to get in and share the story of this universal time encounter, both Jean and Charlie were sobbing and crying uncontrollably. The car was steamy hot with their grief and angst. We were at the intersection of universal time and linear event time; it came to me in that moment very clearly what was going on. We were stepping into a confluence of change, loss, remembrance, and shared misery. Much as stepping into the raging confluence of two rivers— we were emotion-tossed and doing our best to catch our breath as we went under the torrents then came up for air. I actually felt the presence of universal time; my grief of the permanent loss of this earthly relationship with you, which frankly began when you left for Wernersville in 1960 for the Jesuit novitiate, was brought into sharp perspective by the transition of our first son moving off to begin his own independent life away from the family. God was asserting Himself as the only true reality of life and life-giving.

I scuffled in the car amidst the close night air and asked what was going on since going inside the store. Jean and Charlie were embroiled in a tiff and now shared tears and grief. Jean said, "We can't believe how much we are going to miss Thomas!" Charlie echoed the same sentiment as the brother who felt as if he was losing a limb or being cut in half. It was penetrating grief, it touched my inner-most being, possibly my soul; yes, I think it really did touch my soul. My presence in the car stabilized their feelings and they were able to calm down a bit. At which point I related the story of my chance encounter with someone from our (yours and mine) mutual past. I said to them: "Thomas' transition is painful but *not* permanent. We shall see him soon at Thanksgiving or Christmas. When I was in the store, I met a lady that was a friend of Joey and Mary who didn't know that Joe passed away. She reminded me of a more permanent family transition."

Our communal encounter with universal time has stayed with me. It's a story and encounter that has been a spiritual retreat of mine for years. I have shared this story with many others. Most have found it interesting but not as significant as I have over the years. People have difficulty sharing penetrating grief with others. It's not that these feelings and experiences are too thin or wispy such as smoke or fog, but more likely that the presence of the Risen Christ is often confined, maybe even trapped within an illusive tabernacle. At moments like the Giant parking lot experience, the Risen Christ appears a Pillar of Fire for the Hebrews, becomes ever-present, fills the entire space, becomes the very fabric of existence, yet in a way (again within universal time) that we can either embrace His fullness or turn away from that bright revelation which is as lightning. No wonder Paul was blinded!

May 12, 2018: Letter #3—To my brother Joe in Universal Time: The Wrap Up

Dear Joe,

Enjoy this concluding letter for our topic and conversation.

The more I dig into Teilhard and reflect on his presentation and discussion of the Christic, the milieu and the noosphere, the more I encounter again our discussions of universal time. While this topic was not uppermost in the list of things that we discussed during our lunch meetings while I was working at Western Electric on Union Boulevard, Allentown, or when we got together for other shared events, it was a particularly poignant piece of the whole of our talks together. Only

Friday: Long Days, Hard Nights

in the context of universal time can we allow God to be Himself at our expense. Within the restraint of linear event time, we are preoccupied with those things that do have some importance, yet do not "make" our lives the most meaningful. Work, play, rest, communion, all take on the meaning of life only within the context of universal time because they are all so fleeting in linear event time. We take up linear sequenced events with an almost robotic anticipation of the next thing. We look forward more to their ending than to their beginning and their middle!

I recall many of our conversations circling back to an embrace of the really real. My own experience of the Eucharist has become more really real for me as I bring Holy Communion to Jean and those who are disabled in a retirement home. I visited one elderly woman who was a retired nurse and lived in a room at the end of the hall. Hers was a two-room suite with its own bathroom. She was partially blind and would be listening to books on tape when I would come to see her with Communion. She would turn off the tape machine and prepare herself to receive the Eucharist each time. The deliberateness of her actions was striking because it made what I was doing more real. It brought Jesus Christ Himself directly into our midst and suspended the ticking of the clock for a *thicker* time.

In the unfolding timelessness for this Communicant and me, we experienced actions not driven by seconds, minutes, nor by anything of this world. It was a presence, a lived experience. Another lady that I still bring Communion to is a beautiful nonagenarian from New York—Catherine Casey. She is a joy-filled though bed-ridden soul whose beautiful reflection of the Living Christ beams out from a wrinkled face and false teeth. She is the image of universal time. It seems to gush from her whole being. She says she can't understand why she is still alive and waiting for Eternity. *But she says her life remains deeply joyful, almost playful that the Risen Christ has not called her home yet to be with her husband and those she has outlived.*

I have been blessed more than enough to have shared with you, Joe, some wonderful discussions and thoughts and spiritual reflections that I hope give me Catherine's outlook on life no matter how much longer I am alive. I am pushing the envelope of universal time—searching for the Risen Christ. I am both afraid and excited about the prospect of our signal encounter in that great transition.

Please pray for me, my brother, and for every reader!

— *Tom Gossé*

Fast Lunch

I was teaching a social justice course at Holy Name High School, in Reading, Pennsylvania. It was a delight that the text we used cited Joe's booklet, *The*

Spirituality of Work: Unemployed Workers. So I invited Joe down as a guest speaker.

After the morning classes were completed, I invited Joe to the cafeteria for lunch before his presentations to the afternoon sections. Joe politely declined. Since Joe's dietary habits had changed because of medical complications, I did not press the invitation. He said he was going to his car to do some reading and catch-up on paperwork. I then went to the cafeteria for lunch.

After lunch I decided to chat with Joe for a while. Out in the parking lot, there was Joe reclining in the driver's seat, with the local newspaper draped over his body.

"Hey, Joe, what are ya doin'?" I called out.

Removing the newspaper, Joe exposed a gastro feeding tube connected to his stomach. He replied matter of fact and with a slight smile, "Just having lunch."

— *Rev. Thomas J. Orsulak*

The Spirituality of Marriage

Joe had a great prescription for a meaningful and lasting marriage. Simply, spouses should devote themselves daily to an hour of conversation with each other. Joe didn't care where that time together happened. If it meant private time away from the kids, Joe would say, "Go to McDonald's for a Coke." Next on his list for marital success, Joe advocated that couples have one night out every week—a date! Finally, a good marriage includes a romantic weekend away every three months. Joe would give a business twist once in a while and phrase this weekend occurrence as "every quarter." Well, there certainly is a "business" part to every marriage.

Joe's practical elixir was not hard and fast. Yet it was most sensible. He was realistic enough to know that daily hour might be cut short to 15 minutes. Or a given year might only allow one romantic weekend. He simply provided an outline of time where husband and wife would continually get to better know each other through shared conversation.

For marital success and happiness, Joe stood against a "peace at any price" position. He would say, "The two most important words between spouses are not 'Yes, Dear.'" Rather, Joe clearly taught and lived that most significant between husband and wife are the words "Yes" and "No." Joe understood that in order to love your neighbor—and spouses are first neighbors to each other—you must speak your mind clearly. Gray-scale thinking only clouds the topic at hand. In this regard Joe brought Scriptural wisdom into the sacred bonds of marriage: "Say 'Yes' if you mean yes, and 'No' if you mean no" (James 5:12).

Joe knew how and when to say important things about what's important.

Joe's spirituality was formed in deep respect of every vocational state—ordained, married, and single. From first wanting to be a Catholic priest when he was young, he always held a great regard for the Church's "men in black." Disillusionment set in when his bipolar disorder thwarted an 11-year period of formation with the Society of Jesus—the Jesuits. Joe then returned to Pennsylvania's Center Valley from Georgetown.

The Charismatic Movement was nationally vibrant during the latter 20th century. One such community—the Children of Joy—took root in the 1970s at the Allentown College of St. Francis de Sales (now DeSales University). Many of the contributors to this volume knew each other and Joe from Mass, prayer meetings, and social get-togethers. Membership in a Catholic community by souls from the surrounding off-campus area was similar to many Newman Centers at secular college campuses in North America. The faithful went beyond student and faculty populations. Joe's family lived nearby. They helped fortify the community of Christ in the city and countryside.

This is where Joe met Mary Clare, a single mother of three young children. Over a length of time, Joe and Mary formed a close friendship. One day they decided to marry. Joe was completely devoted to his bride, his "diva," as he named Mary Clare. They had written their wedding vows together and prominently displayed these vows in the foyer of their home. Instead of the more common "'til death do us part," Joe and Mary vowed "until the curtain parts." This references the tearing of the Jerusalem Temple's veil upon Jesus' crucifixion (Matthew 27:51). Jesus, in His Seven Sacraments, including Marriage, gives everyone a New Covenant. Joe always presented an alternative to popular culture about marriage. Instead of one spouse trouncing the other, considering unfaithfulness, or stooping to some form of abuse or ridicule, Joe would teach: "Marriage is a great source of freedom." As long as we are not unwisely and unequally yoked (2 Corinthians 6:14), marriage keeps us as free human beings through the presence of our Savior Christ Jesus.

Joe was very clear. "Marriage is a great source of freedom." Rather than emphasizing Saint Paul's admonition that we should not be unequally yoked in any partnership (see 2 Corinthians 6:14–18), Joe exemplified that the primary focus of matrimony is Jesus—then secondarily one's spouse. This ordering leads married couples to increasingly know the Truth of God's Word "which sets us free." So we behold the freedom for loving a spouse or whoever should be the earthly focus of our state in life, versus the opposite of thinking that our freedom lay in running from our ordained or chosen vocation. Marriage, as is each vocational state in life, is not a proposition of enslavement but one of great freedom.

It became evident over many, many years they were very good for each other and marriage was good for their children. As Bill Urbine, who watched everything unfold, observed, "Joe strapped those three kids on his back and became their father."

Joe's father, Joe Sr., firmly influenced his son's respect for women and the Sacrament of Marriage.

Joe Sr. would reinforce with me, "Ronnie, women are different than men. They deserve our complete respect and honor." Joe's youngest brother, Tom, would observe, "Our father always displayed this honor for our mother Margaret. It was like watching the verses of Proverbs 31 lived out in our home."

Before concluding with Joe's poem to his "diva" Mary, let me reminisce about Joe the Elder and Joe the Younger. Joe sometimes referenced the legacy of the father and (adopted) son Pliny from ancient first-century Roman lore—both highly educated and writers. Pliny the Elder was uncle then adoptive father to Pliny the Younger. As history recounts, both Plinys influenced each other similarly to how Joe the Elder and Joe the Younger did: with a love of scholarship, writing, and political contribution. Joe certainly loved the classics for making this comparison!

It was a treasure watching the two Joes greet each other. Both would beam broadly upon a new encounter. Young Joe might say to his father: "Doctor." Joe Senior might quip in response, "Professor." This is how they taught observers to uplift one another by giving an appreciated person a promotion!

Both Gossé men were highly educated. Although neither held an "advanced degree," Joe Senior possessed several patents in metallurgy as an engineer at Bethlehem Steel Corporation in Bethlehem, Pennsylvania. And when someone would engage Joe the Younger in conversation, they might ask: "Where did you complete your

PhD? Joe would always give a mesmerizing answer: "I don't have one!"

Joe Senior and the entire Gossé family were highly involved in welcoming and settling Vietnamese refugees in the Lehigh Valley through our Catholic diocese during the 1970s and '80s. For their family, it was simply a matter of living the Gospel, of loving every neighbor. One refugee from South Vietnam became a Catholic priest in our Diocese—Father Dominic—earning PhDs in astrophysics and pharmacy.

After presenting this poem, published by Joe in his volume, Wellsprings, for his "diva," Mary Clare Gossé shares this lasting tribute from the heart of The Spirituality of Marriage. Their son Todd and daughter-in-law Karen then conclude this section on the ways parental sacramentality influence the next generation's marriage in Christ Jesus.

— Ron Shegda

Ode to Beautiful Mary

O Beauty, Ever Deepening, Wax Melting in Love Drops
>
Of
>
Action: Produced, Directed, Written in the Warm Wind
>
Of Sensitive Love.

Fly, Fly in to Greater Love. Mary No Longer Alone
But with, with Your Joey—Always Companion—Able Always

Friday: Long Days, Hard Nights

To Dissolve Death's Separation: Jesus. Our God of Deepening Love.

Humanize Us.

Ad Maiorem Dei Gloriam—For the Greater Glory of God. Joe lived by this Jesuit motto, where the human soul offers everything up to God!

They said to one another, "Did not our hearts burn within us while he talked with us on the road, while he opened to us the Scriptures?" (Luke 24:32). Before elected as a bishop, Monsignor Ron Gainer commented at a Cursillo Mass that "we don't know if the two disciples on the road to Emmaus were two men or a husband and wife. So this Gospel passage may have very well applied to Joe and me.

The first time I met Joseph Gossé, we talked for three hours. We never stopped talking for the next 36 years. Every evening, until Joe became too weak many years later, we took a walk together. At first we discussed each of our three children. After finishing with the children, we then went over our day. This became a ritual and something we both looked forward to at sunset, nightfall, or bedtime. When Joe passed away in 2000, I tearfully missed our conversations. The loss of our talks together was traumatic for me in the months after Joe's death. I didn't know how I would go on without the input and dialogue which spoke volumes to me and moved me along my journey. Although our values were the same, we did have different points of view; it always helped us hear the other's opinion or have another option. Changing the way we looked at something or shifting our paradigm was crucial in our growth.

Joe not only knew the Scriptures inside and out but lived the Word. Because he lived what he spoke, his words were like fire. I always felt immersed and energized by his interpretation of God's Word. Joe led many Scripture groups both large and small at universities, churches, intimate gatherings, at our parish RCIA, and for inmates at the prison. Every Friday or Saturday evening, and sometimes on Sunday, we hosted a Scripture reflection in our home. We reflected on the upcoming Gospel for Sunday. These reflections prepared us to better receive the Word at Mass on Sunday. An open invitation was extended to everyone. There was usually a core group of regulars along with occasional drop-in guests. We looked forward to the Scripture reflections as the highlight of our week. Many priests and pastors asked Joe to lead Scripture reflections at their parishes. He also spoke about Scripture and led a reflection at Moravian Seminary in Bethlehem, Pennsylvania. Father Larry Hess was teaching at Notre Dame High School when he asked Joe to guide him in how to facilitate a Scripture reflection for students. Joe was always firm about it being a "Scripture reflection" and not a Scripture study, where history and so forth was discussed. Although the study of Scripture is important and needed, he wanted to focus on God's Word and what it means to us in our daily life for each person.

The solemn canonization of Saint Clare took place on August 12, 1255. We chose to marry on the same date many years later.

We wrote to our invited guests: "An invitation is cordially extended, clothed in hope, that you attend St. Paul's Catholic Church, and celebrate the mystery of marriage, mutually gifted by Mary and Joseph on August 12."

Our vows were exchanged as follows:

"Joe, I walk with you during creative periods and fallow periods. I walk with you in mutuality and in brokenness. I join with you in gratitude and receptivity. I join with you in material want and material plenty. I will remain at your side thirsting for the deep truth of union in the Body of Christ until Resurrection is complete."

"Mary, I come not to possess you. I will to give what you will to receive, and I will to receive what you will to give. I deliver to you my word, in challenging times and in more restful times, with Lady Poverty and with Brother Wealth, in tears and amidst delights. I will remain by your side until Christ parts the veil."

For our wedding day, a friend of Joe gave him a suit with a vest. How handsome he donned these clothes! Joe liked the vest very much because it was the first time he ever wore one, and he looked quite dashing. However, when I saw Joe at the altar, I noticed he was not wearing the vest. Later, when I asked what happened to the vest, he sheepishly related the story. A homeless person was begging on the side of the church. Joe spent time talking with the man. The man commented on Joe's attire. The man really liked the vest. The vest was his before the conversation was over—just like John the Baptizer conveys in the Gospel. The man put on the vest and went happily on his way. Although Joe was vest-less when he entered the church, he proved once again to have a very large heart open to the world, especially the poor. Possessions meant very little to Joe. He had what was needed and no more.

Our wedding cake was made by our wonderful Hungarian friend, Elizabeth. Her baking skills were legendary within our family. The top of the cake was done by a couple from our church. It did not include the traditional bride and groom figurines; instead, our nuptial cake presented Saint Francis surrounded by animals.

"See everything. Say little. Overlook much." —Saint Pope John XXIII

This was Joe's motto for raising our children. I remember an instance when we were taking our son to a sporting event. Todd was in the back seat and a discussion came up about something he did which proved a very wrong decision on his part. He said from the rear seat that one of his friends involved in this fiasco was grounded immediately and another had things taken away from him, but our son said that he had to suffer *his* consequences in another way. Joe had a conversation with him and thought, not only should he apologize for his actions with his mother, but he should always be considerate of her and other people. Our son said that others got grounded. Period. Done. But our son's learning from Joe was instead to love, be considerate, and apologize—then think about his actions for the future. I think that pretty much sums up Joe's disciplinary technique.

When I now witness our son's correction of his own children, I am amazed how much his technique mimics Joe's. The placard stating Saint Pope John's words is in my home and I have given a copy to each of the children. Joe wrote articles on everyday spirituality until his last day. These articles have appeared in local, regional, and national publications. Most of his writing was about family and how we can find God in all things and in every situation. We only need to take time to reflect on our experience and discern the meaning of God's will.

> "Three things in human life are important: First is to be kind. Second is to be kind. And third is to be kind." —Henry James

Joe endured kidney dialysis for ten years. Most Americans go to a dialysis center where they receive hemodialysis. They are hooked up to an artificial kidney machine with tubes connected to ports that allow the person's blood to be purified. However, Joe chose peritoneal dialysis. A soft, plastic tube is placed by surgery into the belly. After the filtering process is finished, the fluid leaves the body through a catheter. The person does dialysis while going about their normal activities such as daily work. Joe did this himself for many years. He did it in cars, in hotels, on an airplane, and most anywhere he was on a given day.

Once we took an international flight on Lufthansa Airlines. I was teaching at a high school and we were on a trip with the chorale. When the airline crew heard Joe would be doing dialysis, they brought him up to first class and made him quite comfortable. God saw that the kindness Joe sowed again and again was returned to him many times over. He was able to complete the dialysis with little distraction amidst an atmosphere of privacy and pristine cleanliness. The crew got to know him because he engaged them in conversation; he wrote each one a poem after he learned a little about each of them. On leaving the flight, he was given a bottle of champagne as a special gift to show their appreciation for his poems and for the conversations they had with him. Europeans were much more familiar with the type of dialysis that Joe did and were very accommodating in giving him access to places with extra privacy and cleanliness.

We were soon in London at the Hard Rock Café restaurant with students. I went on a side trip to visit our sister school in Croydon, England. The staff was very helpful to anyone who was on dialysis. The owner was on dialysis and was very considerate with Joe. He was given a suite and access to anything he needed. It seemed that a situation which otherwise might prove difficult was always accomplished with grace, dignity, and a story to relate afterward if Joe was involved. He and the owner were in touch for many years later. For Joe—who harbored an exceptional trait worth replicating—a conversation often led to a meaningful friendship for some time to come.

> "To ignore the suffering of another person is to ignore God." —Pope Francis

I know that Joe would have loved Pope Francis, not just because he's a Jesuit but for what he stands for and how he lives his life. Every time I hear something Pope Francis says or writes, I think Joe is speaking. Our present pope is rooted by *inclusion*, whether it be with the poor, the disenfranchised, or anyone on the fringes of society. Joe would always be found with those whom most people don't want to associate with or be seen with in the public eye. Joe was never embarrassed or ashamed of anyone. He listened to people and truly cared for all people—especially the *anawim* (see Chapter 3). The person befriended by Joe was also changed. Joe was a youth advocate and would take youngsters to get jobs or take them for a meal or simply have a conversation with them. He often brought juveniles home and it made a difference in everyone's lives. No matter how busy Joe was, he always had time for anyone who called or needed to talk to him. He had this in common with Pope Francis. I read accounts that Francis is truly a man of the Gospel instead of a mere church man, someone who genuinely cares about those at the bottom rungs and about our precious common home, the earth. The same quote could also be said about Joe.

True love is an acceptance of all that is, has been, will be, and will not be. Life isn't about how to survive the storm but how to dance in the rain.

Joe could not eat nor drink, not even swab his mouth with water for an entire year. Every night he would be hooked-up to his nutrition device, called "TPN." We would sit down to breakfast, lunch or dinner, and Joe could not partake of anything. I never heard him complain. He was weak and lost lots of weight because of not eating. He went about the year doing what he usually did. He worked, visited the sick, worked with the poor, and yes, had lunch and dinner engagements. He was the happiest and most loving person amidst a life of pain and struggles with his health. Yet he'd be the one who injected humor into a conversation and made others feel good although he was severely struggling himself.

He had something nice to say to everybody. He would lift people from their depression with his smile, his listening skills, and his message of hope and trust in God. Instead of complaining about his many health problems, if someone asked him how he was doing or

Friday: Long Days, Hard Nights

feeling, he would often say he was "tip-top and turning over."

Joe was all about social justice. He wrote letters and called congressmen, senators, and those who influenced change in society. Because of his contact with our local congressman, by phone, e-mail or in person, Joe became acquainted with him, got to know him, and talked with him about many issues facing the country. Joe used to teach friends that in order to influence someone like a congressman—or any person of stature—you must get to know their staff and assistants as well. Joe saw clearly that these people most readily influence the workday of the one you sought to influence. Joe did this out of a genuine Christian "love of neighbor."

It came as no surprise when Joe was asked to be on the congressman's staff as a special assistant. He wrote speeches and sometimes gave speeches for the congressman. He literally had the ear of the congressman. (See Chapters 3 and 4.) Congressman Don Ritter especially prospered in thinking through public policy matters by having Joe pick him up from the airport or drive him from place to place. He deeply appreciated how Joe's knowledge of history, philosophy, and theology rounded out their many conversations concerning the law. Joe was a lifelong old-school Democrat, who tirelessly strived to help the poor and restore a voice to those who had none. He spoke out about racism and was a youth advocate for African-American males, who most of the time had little or no chance of employment. After going to untold places looking for work, many times they would become despondent, but Joe always tried to encourage them and help them with whatever was necessary to secure a job, whether it be more education or gaining skills—such as attending the welding school where Joe had once served as a counselor.

Many of our friends said that Joe was a die-hard liberal working for a conservative Republican. Joe did not like labels. He thought liberals and conservatives could compromise and come together on issues of importance to all. Joe understood liberalism in the classic sense of its meaning, namely "freedom from any oppression or tyranny." His political bias was actually religious because he constantly saw *freedom* as the great goal of any pursuit. He also thought highly of the congressman because he was a scientist, holding a doctorate from MIT, and therefore would look at issues differently than most others and he was open to listening to another approach. Because of Joe's position, he was able to speak with and listen to many politicians while working for the congressman. He influenced politicians by doing research on a particular subject and was able to converse with them on many issues that needed to be addressed. As an experienced writer, Joe could widely extend the audience of his impeccable findings. Many times the politicians were hearing the particular issue from another angle for the first time. Instead of looking at the problem only one way, Joe gave them other options for their thinking.

> "For when the one great scorer comes to write against your name, He writes not if you won or lost, but how you played the game." —Grantland Rice

No one has played the game more eloquently or with more grace and style. Joe's life was a lesson for learning and an inspiration. Simply, Joe's being was a work of art by God.

He read Pierre Teilhard de Chardin, S.J., Bill Lynch, S.J., and Dan Berrigan, S.J., to name a few. He had personal relationships with Bill Lynch, Dan Berrigan, and so many other Jesuits and people of profound learning.

Stop All the Clocks, Cut Off the Telephone
by W.H. Auden

(Some liberty is taken here with additions to Auden's poem. This was read at the cemetery upon Joe's burial.)

> Stop all the clocks, cut off the telephone,
>   Prevent the dog from barking with a juicy bone.
> Silence the pianos and with a muffled drum.
>   Bring out the coffin, let the mourners come.
>
> Let aeroplanes circle moaning overhead,
>   Scribbling on the sky the message *He Is Dead*.
> Put crepe bows round the white necks of the public doves.

Let the traffic policemen wear black cotton gloves.

He was my North, my South, my East and West,
  My working week and my Sunday rest,
My noon, my midnight, my talk, my song;
  Our days flew by quickly; they were not long.

The stars are not wanted now: put out every one.
  Pack up the moon and dismantle the sun.
Pour away the ocean and sweep up the wood.
  My best friend is gone, and Joe was so good.

If I had to summarize Joe's life, it would be as follows: His work was active. He was never a spectator. Joe would tell friends, "We can be in the news . . . or we *make* the news." He walked the walk, the streets of the inner city with the poor. He talked the talk. Then he would walk it once more. He would call and write letters to those who make laws. He appealed to change laws to more keenly reflect the needs of the poor rather than enabling the rich to pay fewer taxes. He changed many people including me, our three children, and myriads of others who were touched by his humility, his faith, and most of all his love for everyone. Joe was a follower of Saint Ignatius. A daily practice of praying the Examen was part of Joe's day.[2] He found God in all things, at every moment, even in the most ordinary circumstances. There are two things most remembered about Joe: his smile and his sense of humor.

Friday: Long Days, Hard Nights

Joe was a poet. His work was published in many periodicals and journals. He wrote this poem about our marriage:

Wedded

From the separate drives
Toward one another,
Over hurdles
  Wrought by emotion,
    Erupting differences—
They state union
Pledge walks
Mark dates
  (coffee, sandwiches)
    Gain entrance—
To mutuality
Cross each threshold.

The two are one,
  Marriage is a working condition
    Created with constancy.

— Mary Clare Gossé

What did I learn, as the middle of three kids, from Joe and our mother, when they married? First, it took a while for me to realize Joe as "the real deal," as my new dad sent from God (like Saint Joseph!), who would protect our mother "in health or sickness, for richer for poorer, to the parting of death." It took us all a while, as any step-family, to see that our mother and Joe entered a real and lasting marriage. There is no such thing as a step-marriage—only a permanent union, with complete fidelity, and open to children. We three kids were already present! [Ed. Note: A memorable observation by Deacon Dr. Bill Urbine, who witnessed Joe and Mary Clare form their life-long bond from the beginning, was this: "Joe strapped all three children on his back and became their father."]

Joe and our mother were married 25 years—until, as Joe wrote for their vows which hung upon our foyer wall these two decades and one-half, "when the veil parts." Joe knew how to relate everything important to Christ. And if it did not relate to Christ, then it was not important. Joe's marriage with our mother demonstrated every day that marriage is a life commitment and a wonderful journey of ups and downs. It's hard work and worth every minute of your time and effort. Marriage is also one of the most rewarding and important relationships in our lives. Joe and my mother created a very special bond, something I never witnessed before. As I watched them, sometimes subconsciously,

Friday: Long Days, Hard Nights

I marveled over their interactions; I witnessed their commitment to each other every day.

Joe, both husband and father in our family, showed how to love by being a servant, by helping others, and by listening. The time they would carve out for each other intentionally was uncanny. I saw it and didn't quite understand it at the time, but now I completely understand. Joe showed me early on how to give actions of love by helping with the dishes, laundry, and taking out the garbage, to name a few mundane chores. I learned this is one of the love languages: being of service. He showed us how to love by being a servant, helping others, and listening. Joe and Mom set boundaries with my sister Roxine, brother Tim, and me, and they made sure they took time for themselves. They would go on spiritual retreats, days of reflection, and were part of a community of faith-filled people. We got to know many from the community and we also became a part of the community because we often hosted many of them at our home. Joe and my mom would spend time walking and talking. This is something Karen and I have adopted. We have two chocolate labs that need a walk every day. I think it's God's sign that we should connect with each other this way. [Ed. Note: See the introduction for this section about Joe's prescription for parsing out marital time during the day, the week, and every three months.]

CONVERSATIONS WITH JOE:
Early on in 1978, Joe would pick me up from baseball practice. I was always amazed at how Joe could listen and be so patient in responding to our conversations. I wasn't the best listener and/or student in middle school or high school. Yet Joe was always there with our mother supporting and encouraging us to do our best. I'm not certain why, but Joe began to call me "Coach." Joe and his family of origin all had a knack for giving appropriate monikers to others. Perhaps Joe recognized that I liked being a team leader in whatever sporting activities I was involved with. I liked being called Coach! It gave me confidence and encouraged me to become better.

Over time, I began to enjoy my conversations with Joe more and more. As the years passed through college and the working world, I appreciated my interactions with Joe even more sweetly. I really looked forward to sitting and having a conversation with him. It seemed like each conversation with Joe was captivating and memorable. Joe was my spiritual yogi or guru—my spiritual advisor! I remember when Joe became very ill in 1996, and I was in mental turmoil living in New York City. I was running in the fast lane and my brakes were not slowing me down. I needed to get out of the rat race and hit the reset button. Mom and Joe invited me to move back to Allentown where we could help out each other. I wanted to be a better man. But how? Ironically, at that same time Karen, my wife to be, called me from Baltimore soon after I moved back to Allentown. We began to date long distance for the next five years. We originally met back in 1992 in Baltimore just after I moved to Metro New York. We went out on a couple of dates but it was not meant to be at that time. It took until 1999 when Karen and I announced that we were getting married in the fall of 2000.

When I had something on my mind, I could really trust Joe as a sounding board. He was the best at listening, asking questions, and engaging in the topic. I remember many of the late-night conversations with Joe where there was no time limit and the conversation was easy flowing, peeling back the onion of whatever topic we were discussing. I never wanted the conversation to end. I believe our interaction was Joe's way of planting the seeds of wisdom and faith in my soul. I saw in Joe the most beautiful, the most spiritual person I have ever known. What did I need to do to become so spiritually connected? Was it more church? More prayer? As these pages convey Joe's practical wisdom for every day, he would advise "all of the above." Yet he would lean toward Scripture.

LOSING MY SPIRITUAL GURU:

When Joe passed away in September of 2000, I was lost. Where would I go to have such deep conversations and gain insight into problems that lay ahead of me? Initially I hadn't taken enough time to reflect on Joe since he left us. However, I always admired Joe's ability to stay present with God every day, no matter what happened. That quality of his humanity has greatly influenced my life.

Throughout the years after Joe passed, I fell and drifted from my spirituality. Now that Joe was gone, I lost hope of ever getting close to the level of spiritual connection I had with Joe. A classmate of Karen's suggested we try the Church of the Nativity in Lutherville, Maryland. Nativity was different than any other Catholic parish I ever attended. Father White was pastor. The church exuded warmth and a welcoming spirit. Father White's sermons struck a chord with me in such a way I felt that he was talking directly to me. I had to carry a handkerchief in my pocket because I was brought to tears so often when I heard the homily. I also found fellowship with other men who were searching for the same thing that I yearned for: the Truth. I was able to connect with a few men's groups that were well-grounded in spiritual awareness. These men spoke the truth and wanted what I wanted, to be the best man I could be through my God. By 2009, I was seeing my father Joe in each one of these men.

Our entire family misses Joe but we also know he is with us. In the many ways we see others, the world, and suffering, it's because of Joe and what he taught us by his life. He was a true Jesuit, a loving husband, and a devoted father.

— *Todd and Karen Benckini*

CHAPTER 7

SATURDAY

THANK GOD IT'S SATURDAY

Go East, Young Man

Horace Greeley, the famed 19th century editor of the New-York Tribune, was known for his memorable headline during America's "manifest destiny" days: Go West, young man, go West.

The Church preceded Greeley's edict. When Saint Paul wanted to bring the Gospel to Asia, the Holy Spirit prevented him (Acts 16). He was instead sent with the other disciples to Greece and Europe. Thomas Merton has commented memorably on how the Church was firmly planted in Europe, then America, and not Asia. All this is notwithstanding how Saint Thomas the Apostle and Saint Francis Xavier have made incredible and lasting beachheads in Southern India, China, and Japan.

Eventually, the Gospel will be firmly present in "all nations... until the end of the age" (Matthew 28:19-20).

Yes. The Church is originally a bequest of the Spirit to the West. She transferred her reign from Jerusalem to Rome—the other city founded on "seven hills." Thereafter France became known as the "first daughter of the Church," given the witness and martyrdom from Saint Denis and Saint Martin of Tours. Joe's spiritual father, Saint Ignatius Loyola, had studied at the University of Paris and formed the Jesuits there.

Although Joe happily married and was a proud father, he considered himself a Jesuit until his last day. He graduated from St. Joe's Prep, a Jesuit high school in Philadelphia, in 1961. Joe's parents, Joe Sr. and Margaret, were good Catholics. Joe's uncle was a priest. So he himself grew up with faithful witnesses for considering the priesthood.

No doubt Joe was deeply influenced by his high school professors. Many of them were members of the Society of Jesus, more familiarly known as the Jesuits. Founded by Saint Ignatius of Loyola (1491-1556), Jesuit tradition profoundly emphasizes education. You could see this borne out by Joe. He constantly had a good book in his hands, continually wrote, and always had something significant to say. Jesuit spirituality is summed up in Ignatius' great work, the Spiritual Exercises. *In them he emphasizes the value of silence, our examination of conscience, and the discernment of spiritual influences. He also guides penitents toward subjecting the faculties of our souls—the intellect, the memory, and the will—to the Trinity and in love of the Church. Joe relished the Jesuit tradition.*

Although his subsequent health dilemmas precluded remaining formally with the Society, Joe maintained lifelong ties. He also remained steeped in reading books written by Jesuits, including Bernard Lonergan, Tielhard de Chardin, Henri de Lubac, John Courtney Murray, Karl Rahner, William Lynch, Anthony de Mello, William Dych, Cardinal Dulles, and Cardinal Martini.

A sign of affection by Joe was if he set the letters "S.J." after addressing your name on an envelope. That meant he considered you a brother or sister. (Joe also conferred many a degree on his letter recipients by conveying the titles Dr., Professor, Honorable, or the like. Sometimes he would set a degree after your name, like STD, PhD, or JD.) He and Mary Clare attended retreats at the Jesuit Center, in Wernersville, Pennsylvania, for many years. They were, in part, Greek mythology Antaeus [1] experiences because Joe completed his novitiate for the Jesuits there. Joe loved Greek connections. After all, Greek civilization is at the root of both Christendom and the West. The Greeks were the parents of Western Civilization.

This next section is by Father Joe Lacey, S.J., who knew Joe at St. Joe's Preparatory School in Philadelphia and at Wernersville's Jesuit Novitiate House of Formation, originally since 1930. The House later transformed into the Jesuit Center for Spiritual Growth, where religious and laity were welcomed for retreats and spiritual direction. Jesuit Novitiate formation proceeded until transfer to Syracuse, New York, in 1993. Here Father Lacey reflects on several significant encounters with Joe—as we might and should do about significant people we meet during life. In the midst of knowing Joe, Father Lacey was given a priestly assignment: Go East. His vocation took him to India.

— Ron Shegda

This book reveals genuine warmth by people, in response to Joe's life. I knew him at the beginning of his high school years. Joe entered St. Joe's Prep in 1957. We were both Philadelphians. I was a senior at the time. As a cheerleader for the football team, I often refereed the freshman touch football games on the great Catholic Feast Days, such as All Saints' Day or the Immaculate Conception. Joe loved the sport and was prominently on the field. Yet this time was only a seedbed of exchange for future years between Joe and me. Reflecting back, it shows that being open, kind, and fair to everyone may provide a meaningful return ten or twenty years later.[2]

After high school graduation I joined the Jesuit novitiate in Wernersville, Pennsylvania. Joe followed me there three years later. Our formation was very monastic—plenty of quiet time, devotion to study, and prayer. We enjoyed a terrific novice master, Thomas Gavigan, S.J. Our lives were tightly organized. After two years of novitiate, I moved over to the other side of the house, the Juniorate. When Joe joined us in 1961, we did not have many opportunities for meeting. The two groups were separated by "grades." Three or four times a year, we would have a "fusion": a soda, pretzel, and potato chip social. That's when we'd talk with those who sat across the dining room or on the other side of the chapel at Mass. We would talk about playing football at the Prep.

These were further nurturing times of getting to know Joe. They again showed me that some meaningful friendships begin very, very slowly. In today's fast-paced world, many of us want relationships to progress almost instantaneously. After Wernersville, I studied philosophy for three years at Shrub Oak, a college of Fordham University in West Chester County, New York. Joe remained in formation at Wernersville. Then in March 1966, I received a teaching assignment at Loyola School in Jamshedpur, India. After that was a time for studying theology at De Nobili College in Poona, India. I was preparing for ordination.

During this time, Joe broke through with a spate of correspondence. He always signed his letters, "Yours in the Sacred Heart of Jesus." One letter particularly impressed Joe's acuity on me when I was in Poona. The year was 1969. Joe broke a significant story about our Maryland Province provincial. I doubted what he said. Then Joe vindicated himself forever with me when a subsequent Time Magazine article presented all the particulars about what Joe told me. Joe was a very sharp commentator on what was significant between two people.

When I visited the States for the first time in nine years in 1975, Joe invited me to dinner with his family of origin. He had concluded his formal eleven-year connection with the Society of Jesus. He already had begun anew with the Children of Joy, a charismatic prayer community in Pennsylvania's Lehigh Valley. Joe thought enough about me to stay in touch all those years. A crowning moment of friendship and hospitality was his awareness about my return home in which he invited me to catch up on all sorts of news at the dinner table.

— *Father Joe Lacey, S.J.*

Inexhaustible Springs

Joe wrote this article for a spiritual publication in 1990. It will ever be current.

Joe was always up-to-date with his secular and spiritual reading, with his work in this world, and the goal of Heaven. Worthy attributes?!? Yes!!!

He loved Stephen Covey's books about excellence in our workaday missions. For instance, in First Things First, *Dr. Covey presents his main teaching: "The main thing is to keep the main thing the main thing." Period. Joe distilled Dr. Covey's books into a blueprint for the seven-day week: Joe spoke about focus days, buffer days, and free days. Buffer days transition us between our hard work of*

Saturday: Thank God It's Saturday

concentration and with a total enlivening of relaxation for our true identity and purpose in life. The goal is to maximize our free days. Not meaning a life of luxury, but a life of wisdom: employing our freedom for the Kingdom of God in Joe's interpretation. Dr. Covey's idea jumped off the pages for Joe almost before the printer's ink dried.

Inexhaustible springs is a favorite Gospel metaphor by Joe from the story of the woman at the well (Saint John, Chapter 4). He also referenced this passage in his book of poetry, Wellsprings.

— Ron Shegda

The young salesman approached the farmer and began to talk excitedly about the book he was carrying.

"This book will tell you everything you need to know about farming," the young man said enthusiastically. "It tells you when to sow and when to reap. It tells you about weather, what to expect, and when to expect it. This book tells you all you need to know."

"Young man," the farmer said, "that's not the problem. I know everything that's in that book. My problem is doing it!"

In a certain sense, the Church, the Bride of Christ, is very much like that young, enthusiastic salesman. The Church is and has been very much aware of the boundless value and beauty of Sacred Scripture since her very beginning. She points to the Scriptures, treasures them, proclaims them, studies them, and teaches them as the living Word of God. The Bride of Christ never ceases to make both the New and Old Testaments available to the Body of Christ.

The Fathers and Doctors of the Church, the saints, popes, bishops, priests, religious, and laity, have always opened God's Word with great joy and immense profit. Their writings testify to this in numerous places. It will suffice for our purpose here to consider a few patristic texts from the Liturgy of the Hours [which is part of the whole cloth of the Mass], and what they tell us about the Word of God.

> Lord, who can comprehend even one of your words? We lose more of it than we grasp, like those who drink from a living spring. For God's Word offers different facets according to the capacity of the listener, and the Lord has portrayed his message in many colors, so that whoever gazes upon it can see in it what suits him. Within it he has buried manifold treasures, so that each of us might grow rich in seeking them out.
>
> The Word of God is a tree of life that offers us blessed fruit from each of its branches. It is like that rock which was struck open in the wilderness, from which all were offered spiritual drink. As the Apostle says: *They ate spiritual food and they drank spiritual drink.*[3]

Saint Ephrem the Syrian compares the Word of God to a living spring, a fabric in many colors, and buried treasure. These descriptions surely and accurately

Saturday: Thank God It's Saturday

portray the nature of Scripture. But they go beyond mere knowledge and information about the Bible, to an indication of the wonderful attractiveness of the sacred books.

After all, what good is it to have a book filled with information, and not be drawn to read it and act on it? The farmer in our story stated the situation very well.

If we are thirsty and we know we are thirsty, coming to a living spring is very attractive. Scripture calls for that awareness of thirst, that sense of dissatisfaction, before the Word of God becomes in reality like a living spring. Usually there is a situation in our lives—perhaps grieving, or sickness, or some form of trouble, that opens to us the thirst that lay beneath the surface of our lives. Then these situations act as paths guiding us unerringly to the source of the living water.

Saint Ephrem continues to speak in terms of various colors, different facets of God's Word, appealing to the capacity of the person listening. This image of various colors opens the door even more widely for us to allow the Word of God into the events of our lives. Our daily realities contain much more than the evil we must endure. There are joyous occasions, times of accomplishment, delights of weather, words and deeds of love by others, acts that call out for gratitude.

This variety of happenings represents a rainbow of colors, suited to many situations and conditions, which fit the gaze of each of us. The Word of God, portraying many facets, can meet us with words and phrases appropriate to everything we encounter. The Gospels, the Psalms, the Wisdom Literature, readily lend themselves to apt reflection on a wide range of circumstances in everyday existence.

The availability of the Word to all that we do and experience means God is being made flesh in our midst, in the tent we have pitched. He is not far; His Word is near.

As we dig deeper through our situations into the dwelling place of the Word of God, Saint Ephrem describes the manifold buried treasures that the sacred books contain. These treasures are such that we dig deep only to uncover richer veins:

> And so whenever anyone discovers some part of the treasure, he should not think he has exhausted God's Word. Instead he should feel that this is all that he was able to find of the wealth contained in it ... Be glad that you are overwhelmed, and do not be saddened because he has overcome you. A thirsty person is happy when they are drinking, and is not depressed because they cannot exhaust the spring. So let this spring quench your thirst, and not your thirst the spring. When you thirst again you can drink from it once more.
>
> What you could not take at one time because of your weakness, you will be able to grasp later if you only persevere. Do not cease

out of faintheartedness from what you will be able to absorb as time goes on.[4]

In these paragraphs, Saint Ephrem offers instructions that lead to *continually drawing waters with joy from the fountain of salvation,* as Isaiah prophetically wrote (12:3). God's Word is an inexhaustible spring of life. We need not nor cannot drain the riches of Scripture in one gulp.

The goal is our return for finding life and nourishment in the Word. The Word of God provides for each situation in our everyday lives. How sorely disappointed we would be in life that if we met Christ Jesus once or twice and concluded we exhausted all He had to offer us!

Scripture provides us with numerous, apparently small openings into the mind and heart of God. These windows are small in order to match the finiteness of our intellects and wills. But the Word meets us *exactly* where we are, just as the disciples on the road to Emmaus were joined in stride by the Risen Christ—who appeared as a stranger. [We can note that the two travelers on the way to Emmaus may have been a husband and wife! Other commentators and certain traditions hold that one of the wayfarers on the road to Emmaus may have been Saint Luke, writer of the fourth Gospel.] They were sad, close to despair, in their limited view of what had just taken place with the death of Jesus, their Leader. But Jesus presents them with words, small words and sentences that relate the words and thoughts of Moses and the prophets right up to Jesus' death and Resurrection.

Through this conversation with the Word of God, about the Word of God, our travelers move from depression and near despair from life's tragic events to... "hearts burning" with encouragement, the vision of faith, the vibrancy of hope, and the fire of love.

It's worth noting these two disciples were not hearing the words of the Old Testament for the first time. In their synagogues the Law and the prophets were read week after week. Now their situation was different. *They are really thirsty,* really stranded and isolated from their hope, their Friend. God's Word seeks such thirsty soil, such parched ground. This is the time of appreciation and deep need. Saint John of the Cross writes to us:

> I reply to all these persons that the Father of lights [James 1:17], who is not close-fisted, but diffuses Himself abundantly as the sun does its rays, without being a respecter of persons [Acts 10:34], wherever there is room—always showing Himself gladly along the highways and byways—does not hesitate or consider it of little import to find His delights with the children of men at a common table in the world [Proverbs 8:31].[5]

Saint Bernard reinforces this relationship between the world of our everyday concerns and activities and

SATURDAY: THANK GOD IT'S SATURDAY

with Christ Jesus, who is the wisdom and power of God:

> Let us work for the food which does not perish—our salvation. Let us work in the vineyard of the Lord and earn our daily wage in the wisdom which says: *Those who work in me will not sin.* Christ tells us: *The field is the world.* Let us work in it and dig up wisdom, its hidden treasure, a treasure we all look for and want to obtain.
>
> *If you are looking for it, really look. Be converted and come.* Converted from what? *From your own willfulness.* "But," you may say, "if I do not find wisdom in my own will, where shat I find it? My soul eagerly desires it. And I will not be satisfied when I find it, and it is not *a generous amount, a full measure, overflowing into my hands.*" You are right. For *blessed is the man who finds wisdom and is full of prudence.*
>
> Look for wisdom while it can still be found. Call for it while it is near. Do you want to know how near it is? *The word is near you, in your heart and on your lips,* provided that you seek it honestly ... If you have found wisdom, you have found honey ... Eat so that you are always hungry. Wisdom says: *Those who eat me continue to hunger.*[6]

In this passage Saint Bernard elaborates on the love of God for the world. "God so loved the world that He gave His only begotten Son" (John 3:16). God's love has not only created the world, but fashioned it as the place, the very field from which we can dig up His wisdom, buried in His Word. We work in the world, we live out our days in the world. Whatever we do for our neighbor, the deeds of love for those close and far, the work and joys and sufferings we bear with one another, all situate us in the broad field that holds God's treasure.

Our activity, prompted and formed by the Word, is all we need do to dig in this field. As we *do* the Word, putting it into practice, the world yields more and more of the real treasure underneath its surface. It is comparable to a mine in which one vein leads us to another, deeper and richer. The treasure we take possession of by reflection and pondering, returns us to those everyday actions we perform for and with our neighbor.

This activity resembles the sifting and washing of metals to discover the gleam and shine of the gold that comes to light. [Ed. Note: Does anyone recall the various goldmining scenes from *The Treasure of Sierra Madre*?] If we are suffering or struggling, the process is like the activity of fire or fast running water as it removes dross and base metal from the precious substance that has been hidden.

God has given us everything. We live in the world, that is our situation. But Scripture reveals that God loves the world so much that His Son has graced it with His presence and will never forsake it. His love is such that the world is a field for our work and play. In the process of doing what we do, we rub this earth with our hands, feet, elbows, and minds. We dig in it continually uncovering the living Word.

The treasure we bring to light itself lights our way back to everyday tasks that bear our names. Unearthed and Heavenly treasure removes our blindness, clarifies our vision, and opens our hearts anew with every neighbor. While our hunger for more wisdom continues, the Word leads us to the Bread of Life that always satisfies.

Saint Bernard summarizes: "*Happy is the man who has found wisdom.* Even more happy is the man *who lives in wisdom,* for he perceives its abundance." [7]

Our eternal life has already begun.

— Joe Gossé

Friendship, Marriage, and a Community of Love

Bob Campanella presents a great conclusion to this volume about conversations with a wise person. Hopefully we all gravitate toward wisdom—one of the Holy Spirit's Seven Gifts (Isaiah 11:1–3). These Gifts are confirmed upon young Catholics at the Sacrament of Confirmation. A special grace in life happens when we truly befriend a wise person, as all of the writers here and untold more did so with Joe.

When the Children of Joy charismatic community migrated from Allentown College (now DeSales University) in Center Valley, Pennsylvania, to St. Paul's parish in nearby Allentown, all sorts of new people met each other. That included Bob and his bride to be, Linda. Joe was an ebullient ambassador of this community and parish—like Saint Paul himself. If you remember from the Preface, I met Joe through Pastor Harry Strassner at St. Paul's when I asked about parishioners interested in social justice. Father Harry referred me to Joe. The rest was history.

St. Paul's parish portrays two most creative and true marquees along Susquehanna Street in Allentown. They read: "St. Paul Catholic Parish. Founded 33 A.D."

— *Ron Shegda*

The year was 1979, on a cold Tuesday evening in February. I was invited to the weekly charismatic prayer community meeting held at St. Paul's parish in South Allentown. The numbers attending were amazing—probably 75 to 100 people filled the social hall. Everyone happily greeted and talked with each other before we formally began. It was obvious that something really important was happening, and we waited with excitement and great anticipation.

Several months earlier I renewed my baptism by re-committing my life to Jesus. This prepared me to learn as much as I could about my Catholic Faith and what it meant to be a friend and follower of Jesus

Saturday: Thank God It's Saturday

Christ. On that first night at St. Paul's, so many people came up and greeted me. This was truly a community of love; it was a place where new friendships would be formed and cherished for many years.

Of course, this was the height of the modern charismatic renewal in the Church, and many prayer communities like St. Paul's were flourishing nationwide. But this night was big, really big! It was here that I would meet so many people who would touch my life in the years ahead. For decades these committed Christians made a lasting impact on my relationship with the Lord. Among those special people were Joe and Mary. When we all met, I learned they were engaged to be married later that summer. Although I had only known them for a short while, I was pleased upon receiving an invitation. I attended their wedding along with many others from the community at St. Paul's. We celebrated and rejoiced as a community in Joe and Mary's new life together.

Joe was an advocate for community. He devoted himself to nurturing those with whom he shared a deep and abiding love for the Savior. Always extending a kind word, combined with both wisdom and a dry wit, Joe would reach out and touch those around him. Either at the prayer meetings, or at other social gatherings, I could always depend on Joe to add a bit of humor and encouragement to any conversation regardless of the place or time. He was always genuinely interested in relating to whatever was happening in our lives. He was a master at keeping any discussion in proper perspective. Joe was seldom anxious about circumstances which would otherwise create fear or frustration for someone else. Rather, he embraced a peaceful acceptance of whatever came his way. Joe precisely lived the Scripture verse: "Be anxious for nothing" (Philippians 4:6). I always hoped this "fruit" would find its way into my life. Joe inspired me to approach challenges and trials with insight and hope.

In his desire for building community, Joe and Mary started a weekly bible study at St. Paul's school. The class was always informal. First we read a Scripture for the upcoming Sunday Mass, followed by group reflection and discussion. Joe kept us on track and offered his own unique insights about what the writer was trying to say. Joe had something for everyone, like a man for all seasons. He would enlighten, persevere, encourage, forgive, be at peace, give thanks, hope, and rejoice. Crowning all these charisms was Joe's gift of love. He would constantly remind us that there was "richness" in the Sacred Scriptures; this richness speaks to our hearts, more deeply and with greater relevance each time we read even the same passage. As our friendship grew over the years, I observed a special holiness about Joe that exuded love and concern for everyone around him. He constantly showed me the love of Christ. This is why people were at peace in his presence.

Saturday: Thank God It's Saturday

Joe could fit in with any group. He would be comfortable addressing any gathering: executives, engineers, hospital workers, prisoners, a congregation, youth, elderly, you name it. The question was whether his audience would fit in with him! It was as if Joe held up a mirror for whomever he addressed. You would get to know who he was, yet more so he would get you to learn something new—especially about yourself. He was truly gifted with a unique manner, kind personality, and with a deep wisdom for discerning the truth in any situation. In our charismatic community, Joe was a solid pillar of strength, surrounded by a gentle and humble exterior that attracted others. Again, Joe was a shining example of living the Scriptures. As St. Paul wrote, "I have become all things to all people, that I might save some" (1 Corinthians 9:22).

Marriage was also a very special community for Joe. He lived within the special graces of this Sacrament. His commitment to Mary and their children was a testimony of his special love for the family. When Linda and I were married in October 1985, Joe and Mary celebrated our union. As a wedding gift, he wrote us a beautiful poem. For over two decades, Joe's poem has hung in our garage. I reflect on it every morning when I leave for work and in the evening when I arrive home again. This was Joe's special gift, and because of his love for us, his words are like a lasting conversation.

Conversations with Joe

"Tender mercies rinsed
    from this gentle man,
        for those standing by the bed of peace,
    his creation
        through consummate union
            achieved.
Now no longer longed for,
    tasted,
    in a new touch,
        as his Creator reaches
    moves in greeting.

What does God look like?
The warm Jewish face of Jesus.
        Whom he met again in so many faces,
    they from far brought near.
        The near drawn closer, even union,
    evenly wrought.

What does God look like?
    For so long
who sees them, sees me."

— Robert A. Campanella

EPILOGUE 1

Joe Gossé was a humanitarian for all, a man for all seasons who inspired people for their full humanity while he was alive, and now also upon departure from this earth. Joe adopted a simple credo for defining and guiding his mature years: Scripture and family. What more significant poles could anyone choose for guiding their journey toward God?

For married people, it can be said their legacy and crowning achievement in life is a quiver of children—full-breathed, loving, wise, and competent with moral direction. (See Psalms 127 and 128.) We already read Joe and Mary Clare's oldest son's reflection, Todd Benckini, about his father's example and influence for marriage. We lengthen our step for concluding this work with short reflections by their oldest and youngest adult children, Tim and Roxine.

— *Ron Shegda*

There are many stories I remember about Joe. He came into our lives, not as someone who tried to change us or to make us conform to his wishes, but as someone who through his gentle manner and sense of humor made us see a different path in life. He became part of our lives because he cared. He took us to sporting events. He encouraged us in our education and was always there to listen to us. I remember writing a college paper that was quite time consuming. Joe was my cheerleader, reading what I wrote and encouraging me until I finished. He always lent his ear when needed. Growing up with the three of us, his ear was needed often! We learned that "ear" is within the very essence of "heart"!!

I recall a time when we were bowling. Bowling was something we liked to do together as a family. Joe made it fun with his sense of humor. No matter how badly I was doing, Joe would always encourage me and kept the positive comments coming. I remember Joe's encouragement the most since his passing. He would always look for the bright side of things even though that is not always easy to do. He had numerous health issues, but complaining was not in his vocabulary. He always tried to look at the bright side of life. I believe that was a special gift he passed on to his children. We should all try to think that way. I hope in some small way that I do try, until this day, to emulate Joe's way of thinking.

— *Tim Benckini, son of Joe Gossé*

My dad Joe loved to sing. He liked Willie Nelson and of course the "King," Elvis Presley. He liked all kinds of music. At that time, I was very young and never heard of these artists. One day, I heard Joe singing "Hound Dog," an Elvis song. Joe sang his heart out to that song.

Epilogue

He just loved singing Elvis songs. I would be sitting and smile and giggle every time he sang. It wasn't until much later in life that I truly appreciated his singing without fear of anybody laughing at him. Joe taught me to "always be myself and never stop smiling." I try to stay true to my father today. During Joe's final moments on earth, I cried and sang gently in his ear "Return to Sender," by Elvis Presley. I hoped that hearing this song would bring some comfort to him as God took him to Heaven. My dad! I love him always!!

*— Roxine Susan Simms,
daughter of Joe Gossé*

EPILOGUE 2: PRAYER TO SAINT JOSEPH

Proclaimed Patron of the Universal Church by Pope Pius IX on December 8, 1870

O blessed Joseph, on whom God bestowed the name and dignity of foster-father of Jesus; and gave Mary ever Virgin to be your most pure spouse; head of the Holy Family on earth; finally chosen by the Vicar of Christ as Patron and Protector of the Universal Church established by the Lord Jesus Christ, with the greatest confidence I implore for that same Church militant on earth, your most powerful assistance. Keep, I beseech you, in the special care of that paternal love with which you burn forever, the Roman Pontiff, all bishops and priests united to the See of Peter. Be the defender of all who labor for the salvation of souls among the sorrows and trials of this life. Bring all peoples of their own free will to submit themselves to the Church, which is everywhere the necessary means of salvation.

Accept, most holy Joseph, the offering of myself, whole and entire, which I make to you, freely and willingly. I consecrate myself wholly to you, to be always my father, protector, and leader in the way of salvation. Obtain for me exceedingly great cleanliness of heart, and a burning love of the interior life. Grant that, following your footsteps, I may direct all my actions to the greater glory of God, in union with the love of the Divine Heart of Jesus and the Immaculate Heart of the Virgin Mary. Finally, pray that I may share in the peace and joy that was yours in your holy death. Amen.

NOTES

Introduction

1. From a spiritual Canticle by Saint John of the Cross. *The Liturgy of the Hours, Vol. I: Advent Season/Christmas Season.* New York, NY: Catholic Book Publishing Co., 1975. p. 1246. (Office of Readings for December 14.)

2. *The Spirituality of Work: Unemployed Workers*, by Joseph Gossé. Chicago: National Center for the Laity/ACTA Publications, 1993.

Chapter 1, "The Sabbath as Pause"

1. *The Little Prince*, by Antoine de Saint-Exupéry. New York: Harcourt & Brace, 1948. First published in France, 1943.

2. *The Spirituality of Work: Unemployed Workers*, by Joseph Gossé. Chicago: National Center for the Laity/ACTA Publications, 1993.

3. See: Matthew 3:1–17; Mark 1:2–11; Luke 1–3; John 1:1–34. This listing follows the order of the

Gospels. It is Saint Luke who writes the fullest story of John the Baptist's conception, birth, and ministry. His parents were Elizabeth and Zechariah.

4. Councils of the Roman Catholic Church, culminating at Trent (1545–1563), accepted the 73 Biblical books originally compiled from Northern Africa as canon. These include 7 books traced to Greek origin, not the original Aramaic. Martin Luther and Protestants accept the 66 books originally from Jerusalem in Aramaic as canon.

Chapter 2, "A New Workweek"

1. Pope Saint John Paul II presents an excellent understanding of work in his encyclical letter, *On Human Work (Laborem Exercens)*. Boston: Daughters of St. Paul, 1981. Especially look for Saint John Paul's description of the three purposes of our work.

2. Ibid.

3. Ibid.

4. All of the books listed in this paragraph are easily available from your favorite supplier. Maybe some or all are even in your home library—ready for re-studying! *The Cloud of Unknowing* is somewhat different as it was written in Middle English by an unknown mystic from the 14th century. Yes, its

author is anonymous! Yet *The Cloud of Unknowing* represents a first expression in English of the soul's quest for God. "A literary work of great beauty in both style and message, it offers a practical guide to the path of contemplation. The author explains how all thoughts and concepts must be buried beneath 'a cloud of forgetting,' while our love must rise toward God hidden in the 'cloud of unknowing.'"

For one of many translations, see: William Johnston. New York: Image Books/Doubleday, 1973.

Bishop-elect Ron Gainer from the Allentown Diocese, who writes in the next chapter, spoke about this "cloud" in a homily on the Solemnity of the Immaculate Conception at St. Theresa parish, Hellertown, Pennsylvania, before he was installed as Lexington, Kentucky's 3rd bishop on February 22, 2003. At the time, Bishop-elect Gainer spoke about the Hebrew wording from Luke's Gospel that "the Holy Spirit will come upon [Mary], and the power of the Most High will overshadow [her] . . . The child to be born will be . . . the Son of God" (Luke 1:35).

Bishop-elect Gainer was most clear that morning: this "overshadowing" by the Holy Spirit is the same phrase written in Exodus 13:21: "The Lord preceded [the Israelites] in the daytime by means of a column of cloud to show them the way . . ."

This is the Cloud of Unknowing which Joe studied closely and which Tom references.

In his exceptional book, *33 Days to Morning Glory*, Father Michael E. Gaitley, MIC, identifies this "Cloud" as the Holy Spirit, the Eternal Immaculate Conception, Who became espoused to Mary, and therefore she took on His Last Name, the Immaculate Conception. This is traditional since Adam and Eve, where God named Adam and Adam named Eve. Mary, the Immaculate Conception, is the New Eve, the Mother of God, Who is Jesus, Who leads us from the bondage of our slavery to sin, to the Promised Land of the Church, the New Israel.

Stockbridge, MA: Marian Press, 2011. pp. 49–64.

Chapter 3, "Listening"

1. Augustine prays, "Lord, let me know myself; let me know you." This is referred to as the "double knowledge"—knowing the Lord and knowing ourselves. All of Christian growth is based on this double knowledge. Augustine of Hippo, *The Confessions of Saint Augustine*, 401 A.D. Translated by Edward Bouverie Pusey, Book I. Idea repeated in opening paragraphs. NY: Collier & Son, 1909. http://www.sacred-texts.com/chr/augconf/aug01.htm

2. Monsignor Romano Guardini, *The Lord*. First published 1937 in German. English edition 1954. Washington, D.C.: Regnery Publishing, Inc.

3. See Matthew 5:3ff, "The Sermon on the Mount" (*The Beatitudes*).

4. Joe relied heavily for spiritual and intellectual inspiration on his mentor, Jesuit Father William Lynch. Father Lynch's most influential book, *Images of Hope*, is subtitled *Imagination as Healer of the Hopeless*. Joe's presentation of himself as a painter was at heart a projection of his creative imagination that aroused hope in others.

See: *Images of Hope*, Notre Dame: University of Notre Dame Press, 1974.

Chapter 4, "A Hard Man Is Good to Find"

1. Louis Bouyer, *Newman: His Life and Spirituality*. New York: P.J. Kennedy & Sons. p. 187. Cardinal Newman never considered himself an eventual saint, like Joe. Both Cardinal Newman and Joe thought themselves ordinary persons and sinners. Yet a plentitude of others considered Cardinal Newman a saint to be. He was beatified by Pope Benedict XVI on September 1, 2010, in Birmingham, England, one step below canonization. Every contributor in this present volume has considered Joe Gossé among the Communion of Saints.

Chapter 5, "Deepening the Spirituality of Work"

1. *The Theology of Marriage & Celibacy*, Pope John Paul II. Boston, MA: Daughters of St. Paul, 1986.

2. Joe loved books like *Everyday Mystic: Finding the Extraordinary in the Ordinary*, by Theresa Joseph. Kindle edition, 2014. Although published after Joe's passing, he was constantly reading and referring books about being a contemplative in a secular and everyday world.

Chapter 6, "Long Days, Hard Nights"

1. See Pierre Teilhard de Chardin, *The Phenomenon of Man*. New York, NY: Harper Torchbooks, The Cloister Library, Harper & Row Publishers, 1961. (First published in French, 1955.) Also see *The Divine Milieu*. New York, NY: Harper & Row, 1960. (First published in French, 1957).

2. *The Spiritual Exercises of St. Ignatius Loyola*, Translated by Thomas Corbishley, S.J. Wheathampstead, Hertfordshire, Great Britain: Anthony Clarke Books, 1963.

Notes

Chapter 7, "Thank God It's Saturday"

1. Joe loved metaphors and puns—any good play on words, especially if there was an Ancient Greek reference. Antaeus was a figure in Greek Mythology known for his wrestling prowess. He acted invincibly as long as he remained in contact with his mother, the earth (Gaia). Greek wrestling, like its modern equivalent, forced opponents to the ground. This was the secret of Antaeus' continued success.

    Here's the point of the current metaphor: There is good and bad in everything: a potential of loss or gain. Joe grappled with these good and bad turning points his entire life—as we are all called to do. For Joe, the Jesuit experience represented both a success and a failure. It was similar for Antaeus, who ended up wrestling with Heracles. Heracles realized he could not beat Antaeus by throwing or pinning him. Instead, he held him aloft and held victory in his arms.

2. Joe loved football throughout his adult life. A particular idiosyncrasy is that he would call a "field goal" a "fielder." The spirit of football lived in the Gossé home. When Joe's adult son, Todd, would visit when his brother Tom and Tom and Jean's two boys were there, Todd would drop to a three-point stance in the living room opposite Thomas and Charles, simulating a football snap. It was fantastic to see!

3. "Commentary on Diatessaron," by St. Ephrem. *The Liturgy of the Hours, Vol. III: Ordinary Time, Weeks 1–17.* New York, NY: Catholic Book Publishing Co., 1975. p. 200. (Office of Readings for Sixth Sunday in Ordinary Time.)

4. Ibid. pp. 199–200.

5. *Living Flame of Love: The Collected Works of St. John of the Cross*, Edited by Kiernan Kavanaugh and Otilio Rodriguez, 2nd edition. Washington, D.C.: ICS Publications, 1979. pp. 584–5.

6. "Sermon by St. Bernard of Clairveaux." *The Liturgy of the Hours, Vol. III: Ordinary Time, Weeks 1–17.* Ibid. pp. 203–4. (Office of Readings for Monday of the Sixth Sunday in Ordinary Time.)

7. Ibid. p. 204.

About the Editor

Ron Shegda lives in Pennsylvania's Lehigh Valley and is a layman in the Catholic Diocese of Allentown. His master's thesis, *The Regenerative Economy*, was published by Rodale Press. Ron was a graduate of the University of Pennsylvania and Tufts University. His articles and editorials have appeared in numerous religious and secular publications over the years.

About Leonine Publishers

Leonine Publishers LLC makes fine Catholic literature available to Catholics throughout the English-speaking world. Leonine Publishers offers an innovative "hybrid" approach to book publication that helps authors as well as readers. Please visit our web site at www.leoninepublishers.com to learn more about us. Browse our online bookstore to find more solid Catholic titles to uplift, challenge, and inspire.

Our patron and namesake is Pope Leo XIII, a prudent, yet uncompromising pope during the stormy years at the close of the 19th century. Please join us as we ask his intercession for our family of readers and authors.

Do you have a book inside you? Visit our web site today. Leonine Publishers accepts manuscripts from Catholic authors like you. If your book is selected for publication, you will have an active part in the production process. This book is an example of our growing selection of literature for the busy Catholic reader of the 21st century.

www.leoninepublishers.com

www.ingramcontent.com/pod-product-compliance
Lightning Source LLC
Chambersburg PA
CBHW032357040426
42451CB00006B/40